The Revival We Need

by

Oswald J. Smith

www.solidchristianbooks.com

2015

Contents

Preface

Five years ago there came into my life a spiritual experience that revolutionized my work, and resulted in a Ministry characterized by some of the manifestations that usually accompany Revivals.

It was in this atmosphere that these messages were born; and while the writing of them has occupied the five intervening years, they but breathe the spirit that then prevailed.

May God through them reveal to His servants the shallowness apparent in so much of our Modern Evangelism, and turn them to that deep and abiding work of the Holy Spirit which will alone stand the test of divine fire!

Oswald J. Smith

Toronto, 1922

Foreword by Jonathan Goforth

MR. SMITH'S book, "The Revival We Need," for its size is the most powerful plea for revival I have ever read. He has truly been led by the Spirit of God in preparing it. To his emphasis for the need of a Holy Spirit revival I can give the heartiest amen. What I saw of revival in Korea and in China is in fullest accord with the revival called for in this book.

It is most timely that Mr. Smith has called attention to man effort and man method in modern revival. If we all had faith to wait upon God in intense believing prayer there would be genuine Holy Ghost revival, and the living God would get all the glory. In Manchuria and China, when we did nothing else than give the address and let the people pray, and kept out of sight as far as possible, we saw the mightiest manifestations of Divine power.

Had I the wealth of a millionaire I would put "The Revival We Need" in every Christian home on this continent and confidently look for a revival which would sweep round the world.

JONATHAN GOFORTH.

Toronto, May 5, 1925

CHAPTER 1 THE OUTPOURING OF THE SPIRIT

IT was in 1904. All Wales was aflame. The nation had drifted far from God. The spiritual conditions were low indeed. Church attendance was poor. And sin abounded on every side.

Suddenly, like an unexpected tornado. the Spirit of God swept over the land. The Churches were crowded so that multitudes were unable to get in. Meetings lasted from ten in the morning until twelve at night. Three definite services were held each day. Evan Roberts was the human instrument, but there was very little preaching. Singing, testimony, and prayer, were the chief features. There were no hymn books; they had learnt the hymns in childhood. No choir, for everybody sang. No collection; and no advertising.

Nothing had ever come over Wales with such far-reaching results. Infidels were converted, drunkards, thieves, and gamblers saved; and thousands reclaimed to respectability. Confessions of awful sins were heard on every side. Old debts were paid. The theatre had to leave for want of patronage. Mules in the coal mines refused to work, being unused to kindness. In five weeks 20,000 joined the Churches.

In the year 1835 Titus Coan landed on the shore belt of Hawaii. On his first tour multitudes flocked to hear him. They thronged him so that he had scarcely time to eat. Once he preached three times before he had a chance to take breakfast. He felt that God was strangely at work.

5

In 1837 the slumbering fires broke out. Nearly the whole population became an audience. He was ministering to 15,000 people. Unable to reach them, they came to him, and settled down to a two years' camp meeting. There was not an hour day or night when an audience of from 2,000 to 6,000 would not rally to the signal of the bell.

There was trembling, weeping, sobbing, and loud crying for mercy, sometimes too loud for the preacher to be heard; and in hundreds of cases his hearers fell in a swoon. Some would cry out, "The two edged sword is cutting me to pieces." The wicked scoffer who came to make sport dropped like a dog, and cried, "God has struck me !" Once while preaching in the open field to 2,000 people, a man cried out, "What must I do to be saved?" and prayed the publican's prayer, and the entire congregation took up the cry for mercy. For half an hour Mr. Coan could get no chance to speak, but had to stand still and see God work.

Quarrels were made up, drunkards reclaimed, adulterers converted, and murderers revealed and pardoned. Thieves returned stolen property. And sins of a lifetime were renounced. In one year 5,244 joined the Church. There were 1,705 baptised on one Sunday. And 2,400 sat down at the Lord's table, once sinners of the blackest type, now saints of God. And when Mr. Coan left he had himself received and baptised 11,960 persons.

In the little town of Adams across the line, in the year 1821, a young lawyer made his way to a secluded spot in the woods to pray. God met him there and he was wondrously converted, and soon after filled with the Holy Spirit. That man was Charles. G. Finney.

The people heard about it, became deeply interested, and as though by common consent, gathered into the meeting house in the evening. Mr. Finney was present. The Spirit of God came on them in mighty, convicting power, and a Revival started. It then spread to the surrounding country until finally nearly the whole of the Eastern States was held in the grip of a Mighty Awakening. Whenever Mr. Finney preached the Spirit was poured out. Frequently God went before him so that when he arrived at the place he found the people already crying out for mercy.

Sometimes the conviction of sin was so great and caused such fearful wails of anguish that he had to stop preaching until it subsided. Ministers and Church members were converted. Sinners were reclaimed by thousands. And for years the mighty work of grace went on. Men had never witnessed the like in their lives before.

I have recalled to your minds three historical incidents of the Outpouring of the Holy Spirit. Hundreds of others might be cited. But these are sufficient to show what I mean. And this is what we need today more than anything else. When I remember that such an Outpouring has come to China, India, Korea, Africa, England, Wales, the States, the Islands of the Seas, and many other places, but that Canada, our Dominion, our own beloved country, has never in its history experienced a national Revival, my heart cries out to God for such a Manifestation of Himself.

Do we need it? Listen! How many of our churches are more than half empty Sunday after Sunday? What a multitude there are who never enter God's house? How many mid-week prayer meetings are alive and prosperous? Where is the hunger for spiritual things? Oh, the shame of it!

And Missions--the lands beyond the seas, heathen darkness--what are we doing? Does the fact that multitudes are perishing ever cause us an anxious thought? Have we grown selfish?

What about the tremendous wealth that God has given us? Take the United States as an example, the richest nation in the world today, and the major portion of her wealth in the hands of professing Christians. And yet the United States spent more on gum in one year than she spent on Missions. How many Christians are giving God even the tenth of what He gives them?

Then take our colleges and seminaries, both at home and on the mission field where higher criticism is taught. We are told that Jesus never performed any miracles, never rose from the dead, and was not born of a virgin, did not die as our Substitute, and is not coming again. Oh, what blasphemy!

How many professing Christians are living the Christ-life before men? Oh, how like the world we are becoming! How little opposition do we find! Where are the persecutions that were heaped on the Early Church? How easy it is now to be a Christian!

And what of the Ministry? Does the minister grip, convert, and save by his message? How many souls are won through the preaching of the Word? Oh, my friends, we are loaded down with countless Church activities, while the real work of the Church, that of evangelizing the world and winning the lost, is almost entirely neglected.

Where is the conviction of sin we used to know? Is it a thing of the past? Let us look at one of Finney's meetings. Oh, that we could repeat it today! He tells us that one time when he was conducting meetings in Antwerp, an old man invited him to preach in a small school house near by. When he arrived the place was packed so that he could barely find standing room near the door. He spoke for a long time. At last he began to press home upon them the fact that they were an ungodly community; for they held no services in their district. All at once they were stricken with conviction. The Spirit of God came like a thunderbolt upon them. One by one they fell on their knees, or prostrate on the floor, crying for mercy. In two minutes they were all down, and Mr. Finney had to stop preaching for he was unable to make himself heard. At last he got the attention of the old man who was sitting in the middle of the room and gazing around him in utter amazement, and shouted to him at the top of his voice to pray. Then taking them one by one he pointed them to Jesus. The old man took charge of the meeting while he went to another. All night it continued, so deep was the conviction of sin. The results were permanent, and one of the young converts became a most successful minister of the gospel.

Ah, yes, men have forgotten God. Sin flourishes on every side. And the pulpit fails to grip. And I know of nothing less than the Outpouring of His Spirit that can meet the situation. Such a Revival has transformed scores and hundreds of communities, it can transform ours.

Now, how may we secure such an Outpouring of the Spirit? You answer, by prayer. True, but there is something before prayer. We will have to deal first of all with the question of sin; for unless our lives are right in the sight of God, unless sin has been put away, we may pray until doomsday, and the Revival will never come. "Your iniquities have separated between you and your God, and your sins have hid His face from you so that He will not hear." (Isa. 59: 2.)

Probably our best guide just here is the prophecy of Joel. Let us look at it. It is a call to repentance. God is anxious to bless His people, but sin has withheld the blessing. And so in His love and compassion He brings a fearful judgment upon them. We have it described in chapters 1 and 2. It has almost reached the gates of the city. But see--how great is His love! Notice verses 12-14 of chapter 2, where He says, "Turn ye even to Me with all your heart, and with fasting, and with weeping, and with mourning; and rend your heart, and not your garments, and turn unto the Lord your God; for He is gracious and merciful, slow to anger, and of great kindness, and repenteth Him of the evil. Who knoweth if He will turn and repent, and leave a blessing behind Him?"

Now my friend, I don't know what your sin is. You know and God knows. But I want you to think about it, for you may as well stop praying and rise from your knees until you have dealt with it, and put it away. "If I regard iniquity in my heart, the Lord will not hear me." Let God search your heart and reveal the hindrance. Sin must be confessed and put away.

It may be you will have to forsake some *P.65* cherished idol. It may be you will have to make restitution. Perhaps you are withholding from God, robbing Him of His own. But this is your affair, not mine. It lies between you and God.

Now notice verses 15-17. The prophet has called for a prayer meeting. Sin has been confessed and forsaken. Now they may pray. And they are to entreat God for His own name's sake, lest the nations say, "Where is their God?" They are dead in earnest now and their prayer is going to prevail. Listen! "Blow the trumpet in Zion, sanctify a fast, call a solemn assembly: gather the people, sanctify the congregation; assemble the elders, gather the children. Let the priests, the ministers of the Lord, weep between the porch and the altar, and let them say, "Spare Thy people, O Lord, and give not Thine heritage to reproach, that the heathen should rule over them: wherefore should they say among the people, "Where is their God?"

Ah! my brethren, are you praying? Do you plead with God for this city? Are you beseeching Him night and day for an Outpouring of His Spirit? For now is the hour to pray. We are told of a time in the work of Finney when the Revival had died out. He then made a covenant with the young people to pray at sunrise, noon and sunset in their closets for one week. The Spirit was poured out, and before the week ended the meetings were thronged.

And of course it must be believing prayer, prayer that expects. If God stirs up hearts to pray for a Revival it is a sure sign that He wants to send one and He is always

11

true to His Word. "There shall be showers of blessing."
His promises never fail. Have we faith? Do we expect an
Awakening?

Now notice the speedy answer in verse 18. "Then!" After
they had forsaken sin and cried unto God in prayer.
"Then will the Lord be jealous for His land, and pity His
people." The answer is not long in coming once the
conditions have been met. We have it fully described in
verses 28-29: "And it shall come to pass afterward, that
I will pour out my Spirit upon all flesh; and your sons
and your daughters shall prophesy, your old men shall
dream dreams, your young men shall see visions; and
also upon the servants and upon the hand-maids in
these days will I pour out my Spirit."

Oh, my brethren, the trouble is not with God. It lies right
here with ourselves. He is willing, more than willing. But
we are not ready. And He is waiting for us. Are we going
to keep Him waiting long?

DEAL W/SIN

PRAY
EXPECT / BELIEVE

CHAPTER II THE RESPONSIBILITY FOR REVIVAL

AS far back as I can remember my heart has burned within me whenever I have heard or read accounts of the mighty work of God in the great Revivals of past years. The heroic missionaries of the cross in foreign lands, and the lonely men of God in the home field around whom these gracious Visitations have centered, have always been a source of untold inspiration to my life. David Brainerd, Adoniram Judson, Chas. G. Finney, Robt. Murray McCheyne--these and many others have been my bosom companions and friends. I have watched them, listened to them, lived with them, until I have almost felt the spirit of the atmosphere in which they moved. Their trials and hardships, their prayers and tears; their joys and sorrows, their glorious triumphs and victorious achievements have thrilled my very soul until I have fallen down upon my face and exclaimed with the prophet of old: "Oh, that Thou wouldst rend the heavens, and that Thou wouldst come down !" The great Awakening of the 18th century under John Wesley, the stirring Irish Manifestation of 1859, the glorious American Visitation in the 19th century under Chas. G. Finney, and in our own day the mighty Welsh Revival of 1904-05--Manifestations such as these have been my meat and drink for years past. I have heard again the uncontrollable sob and groan of the convicted, the exceeding bitter cry of the penitent, and the unspeakable expressions of joy of the delivered. And I have sighed within myself for another such Manifestation of God's presence and power.

From my boyhood it has been my delight to read more or less of God's work along these lines, but lately I have been led to lay all else aside and to literally devour everything I could lay hands on regarding Revival work. And as I studied the lives of those whom God has signally used all down the centuries, especially the labors of the Puritans, the early Methodists and others of later years, and saw how wonderfully they were owned of Him--how they worked for, expected and got what they sought --I was compelled to admit that I saw nothing like it today either in my own ministry or in the ministry of others. The average church does not aim at, let alone get, results. Men preach and never even dream of anything happening. Oh, how far away we have drifted! How powerless we have become!

It is reported that there were 7,000 churches that did not win a single soul for Jesus Christ in an entire year. That means that 7,000 ministers preached the Gospel for a whole year without reaching even one lost soul. Supposing that they preached, putting it at a low average, on 40 Sundays, not including extra meetings, that would mean that these 7,000 ministers preached 560,000 sermons in a single year. Think of the work, the labor, the money expended in salaries, etc., to make this possible. And yet 560,000 sermons preached by 7,000 ministers in 7,000 churches to tens of thousands of hearers during a period of twelve months, failed to bring a single soul to Christ.

Now, my brethren, there is something radically wrong somewhere. There is either something the matter with these 7,000 ministers or else with their 560,000 sermons, or with both.

In reading over the Twelve Rules of the Early Methodist church I was struck with the fact that they aimed at and looked upon soul-winning as their supreme task. Let me quote from one of them: "You have nothing to do but to save souls. Therefore spend and be spent in this work. It is not your business to preach so many times; but to save as many souls as you can; to bring as many sinners as you possibly can to repentance, and with all your power to build them up in that holiness, without which they cannot see the Lord."--From "The Twelve Rules."-- John Wesley.

The practical application of this rule is demonstrated in the life of Wm. Bramwell one of their most remarkable men. "He was not, as the words are commonly understood, a great preacher. But if that man is the best physician who performs the most cures, that is the best preacher who is the instrument of bringing the greatest number of souls to God; and in this view Mr. Bramwell will be entitled to rank amongst the greatest and best Christian ministers."--Memoir of Wm. Bramwell.

John Oxtoby was so used of God that he was able to say: "I am witnessing daily the conversion of sinners, I seldom go out but God gives me some Fruit."

It was said of John Smith, one of their most wonderfully anointed men and the spiritual father of thousands, that "he ceased to estimate all preaching, and indeed all ministerial labor except as it produced saving effects. 'I am determined by the grace of God to aim at souls,' he exclaimed. 'A minister of the Gospel is sent to turn men from darkness to light, and from the power of Satan to God!' Of that species of preaching which only produced intellectual pleasure, he had a holy abhorrence. Nothing can be more characteristic of the man than his remark to a friend, on sermons in which power of intellect or imagination is almost exclusively predominant: 'They achieve nothing, Sir.' "--Life of John Smith.

"I cannot tell how they get their time over who can drag on and see no Fruit. Were that so in my case I should be ready to conclude that I was out of my place."--Thos. Taylor.

"If your hearts be not set on the end of your labors, and you do not long to see the conversion and edification of your hearers, and do not study and preach in hope, you are not likely to see much fruit of it. It is an ill sign of a false, self-seeking heart, that can be content to be still doing, and see no fruit of their labor."--Richard Baxter.

Then I compared the results of my ministry with the promises of God. In Jet. 23:29, I read: "Is not My Word like a Fire, saith the Lord; and like a Hammer that breaketh the rock in pieces?" And in Eph. 6:17, "The Sword of the Spirit, which is the Word of God." But the more I pondered over it, the more I was convinced that in my ministry the Word of God was not a Fire, a Hammer, and a Sword. It did not burn, break and pierce. There was no execution. Heb. 4:12, declares that "the Word of God is quick and powerful, and sharper than any two edged sword, piercing even to the dividing asunder of soul and spirit, and of the joints and marrow,

16

and is a discerner of the thoughts and intents of the heart." I had never seen it so. John Wesley saw it. John Smith was a constant observer of it. David Brainerd witnessed its sharpness; but I did not. "So shall My Word be that goeth forth out of my mouth; it shall not return to me void, but it shall accomplish that which I please, and it shall prosper in the thing whereto I sent it." (Isa. 55:11.) And I knew that this wonderful promise had not been fulfilled in my preaching. I had no evidence such as Paul, Wm. Bramwell and Chas. G. Finney that it did not return void many and many a time. And I had a right to the evidence. Was it any wonder that I began to challenge my preaching?

And not only my preaching, but my prayer life as well. This also had to be challenged and tested by the Outcome. And I was forced to admit that the confident assertion of Jer. 33:3, "Call unto Me, and I will answer thee, and show thee great and mighty things, which thou knowest not," was not realized in my experience. The "great and mighty things" were almost daily witnessed by Evan Roberts, Jonathan Goforth and others, but not by me. My prayers were not definitely and daily answered. Hence, John 14:13-14, "Whatsoever ye shall ask in My name, that will I do," and "If ye shall ask anything in My name, I will do it," was not real in my case. To me these promises were not vital since I asked for many things that I did not receive, and this was not according to the promise.

Thus I came to realize that there was something radically wrong with my prayer-life. And in reading the autobiography of Chas. G. Finney, I found that he, too, had experienced the same failure. "I was particularly struck," he relates, "with the fact that the prayers that I had listened to, from week to week, were not, that I could see, answered. Indeed, I understood from their utterances in prayer, and from other remarks in their meetings, that those who offered them did not regard them as answered.

"They exhorted each other to wake up and be engaged, and to pray earnestly for a Revival of religion, asserting that if they did their duty, prayed for the outpouring of the Spirit, and were in earnest, that the Spirit of God would be poured out, that they would have a Revival of religion, and that the impenitent would be converted. But in their prayers and conference meetings they would continually confess, substantially, that they were making no progress in securing a Revival of religion.

"This inconsistency, the fact that they prayed so much and were not answered, was a sad stumblingblock to me. I knew not what to make of it. It was a question in my mind whether I was to understand that these persons were not truly Christians. and therefore did not prevail with God; or did I misunderstand the promises and teachings of the Bible on this subject, or was I to conclude that the Bible was not true? Here was something inexplicable to me, and it seemed, at one time, that it would almost drive me into scepticism. It seemed to me that the teachings of the Bible did not at all accord with the facts which were before my eyes.

"On one occasion, when I was in the prayer meeting. I was asked if I did not desire that they should pray for me. I told them no, because I did not see that God answered their prayers. I said, 'I suppose I need to be prayed for, for I am conscious that I am a sinner; but I do not see that it will do any good for you to pray for me; for you are continually asking, but you do not receive. You have been praying for a Revival of religion ever since I have been in Adams, and yet you have it not.'"

When John Wesley concluded his message he cried to God to "confirm His Word," to "set to His Seal," and to "bear witness to His Word." And God did. Sinners were stricken immediately, and began to cry for mercy under fearful conviction of sin, and soon after, in a moment they were set at liberty, and filled with unspeakable joy in the knowledge of a present Salvation. In his wonderful journal he sets down what his eyes witnessed, and his ears heard in the following words:

"We understood that many were offended at the cries of those on whom the power of God came; among whom was a physician, who was much afraid there might be fraud or imposture in the case. Today one whom he had known many years was the first who broke out in strong cries and tears. He could hardly believe his own eyes and ears. He went and stood close to her, and observed every symptom, till great drops of sweat ran down her face, and all her bones shook. He then knew not what to think, being clearly convinced it was not fraud, nor yet any natural disorder. But when both her soul and body were healed in a moment, he acknowledged the finger of God."

Such was also the experience of the Early Church. "Now when they heard this they were pricked in their hearts, and said unto Peter and to the rest of the Apostles, men and brethren, what shall we do?" (Acts 2:37.) Long time therefore abode they speaking boldly in the name of the Lord, which gave testimony unto the Word of His grace, and granted signs and wonders to be done by their hands." (Acts 14:3.) They prayed "that signs and wonders" might "be done." (Acts 4:30.) And Paul declared that the Gospel is "the power of God unto Salvation." (Rom. 1:16.) Yet all this was utterly foreign to my work.

In the Irish Revival of 1859, "signs and wonders" were seen on every side. Among the Early Methodists they were of daily occurrence. But with me the Gospel was not "the power of God unto Salvation." God did not "confirm His Word," "set to His seal," or "bear witness to His Word," when I preached. And I knew I had the right to expect it for Jesus Himself had given the promise. "The works that I do," He declared, "shall ye do also and greater works than these shall ye do." (John 14:12.)

Then one day I read the Acts of the Apostles to find out if God's servants in the Early Church got results wherever they went. And I found as I read that they aimed at, worked for, expected, and never failed to get Fruit. Peter preached on the day of Pentecost and 3,000 responded to that first appeal. There was a definite Outcome. With Paul it was the same. Follow him from place to place, and wherever he goes churches spring up. See how repeatedly the results are noted throughout the book. "They were added unto them about 3,000 souls." (2:41.) "Many of them which heard the Word believed, and turned unto the Lord." (11:2.) "Much people was added unto the Lord." (11: 24.) "A great multitude believed." (11: 1.) "Some believed, of the devout Greeks a great multitude, and of the chief women not a few." (17:4.) "Many believed." (17:34.) "Some believed." (28:24.)

And Paul was able to declare "what things God had wrought by His Ministry." (21: 19.)

Oh, how far short I fell! How fearfully I had failed! failed in the very thing for which God had called me into the Ministry. How seldom I could write after having preached that "a great number believed and turned unto the Lord," or even that "some believed." Nor was it possible for me to declare with Paul "what things God had wrought by my Ministry."

God clearly and emphatically states that it is His will that every servant of His should bear Fruit. "I have chosen you and ordained you," he affirms, "that ye should go and bring forth Fruit." (John 15:16.) Too long was I content to sow and evangelize, using the excuse that I left the results with God, thinking I had then done my duty. When people are saved and greatly blessed they will say so, and if they don't there is reason to doubt the reality of an Outcome. George Whitefield sometimes received hundreds of letters after he had preached telling of blessing and conversions.

"Go into the public assembly with a design to strike, and persuade some souls there, into repentance and salvation. Go to open blind eyes, to unstop deaf ears, to make the lame walk, to make the foolish wise, to raise those that are dead in trespasses and sins to a Heavenly and Divine life, and to bring guilty rebels to return to the love and obedience of their Maker, by Christ Jesus the great Reconciler, that they may be pardoned and saved. Go to diffuse the saviour of Christ and His gospel through a whole assembly and to allure souls to partake of His grace and glory."--Dr. Watts.

21

There are men who feel they have special talents for the edification of believers, and so they give themselves entirely to building up Christians in the Faith. This was where I was side-tracked. I felt that I had special gifts for teaching and speaking to young Christians on the Deeper Life, and so I prepared a number of addresses with the idea of devoting my time to this work, until God mercifully opened my eyes and showed me how far I was astray. There is nothing that will deepen Christian experience, edify believers and build them up in the Faith so rapidly and thoroughly as seeing souls saved. Deep Holy Spirit meetings where the power of God is working mightily in the conviction and Salvation of sinners will do more for Christians than the teaching of years without it. Such was the experience of David Brainerd. In writing of the Indians among whom he labored he says, "Many of these people have gained more doctrinal knowledge of Divine truths since I have first visited them in June last, than could have been instilled into their minds by the most diligent use of proper and instructive means for whole years together, without such a Divine influence."

An incident is related of Wm. Bramwell: "Several local preachers," it states, "had said that their talents were not to awaken and arouse careless and impenitent sinners, but to build up believers in the Faith. Mr. Bramwell endeavoured to prove that such reasoning was frequently used as an apology, for the loss of the life and powers of God. That although some preachers might have a peculiar talent for comforting and edifying believers, yet that Christ's true servants, those whom He sent into His vineyard, could do all sorts of work. They could plough, dig, plant, sow, water, etc., and he earnestly entreated the preachers not to be satisfied without seeing the fruit of their labors, in the awakening and conversion of sinners."

"The building up of believers in their most Holy Faith was a principal object of Mr. Smith's ministry; but he never considered this species of labor successful, except as its results were indicated in the conversions of sinners."-- Life of John Smith.

"He most certainly and perfectly edifies believers who is most ardently and scripturally laborious for the conversion of sinners."--Life of John Smith.

Work among believers of itself will not suffice. It matters not how spiritual a church may profess to be, if souls are not saved something is radically wrong, and the professed spirituality is simply a false experience, a delusion of the devil. People who are satisfied to meet together simply to have a good time among themselves, are far away from God. Real spirituality always has an Outcome. There will be a yearning and a love for souls. We have gone to places that have a name of being very deep and spiritual, and have often found that it was all in the head, the heart was unmoved; and there was, not infrequently, hidden sin somewhere. "Having a form of Godliness but denying the power thereof." Oh, the pathos of it all! Let us then challenge our spirituality and ask what it produces; for nothing less than a genuine Revival in the Body of Christ resulting in a true Awakening among the unsaved will ever satisfy the heart of God.

CHAPTER III SOUL-TRAVAIL

WE read in Isa. 66:8, that "as soon as Zion travailed she brought forth her children;" and this is the most fundamental element in the work of God. Can children be born without pain? Can there be birth without travail? Yet how many expect in the spiritual realm that which is not possible in the natural! Oh, my brethren, nothing, absolutely nothing short of soul-travail will bring forth spiritual children! Finney tells us that he had no words to utter, he could only groan and weep when pleading with God for a lost soul. That was true travail.

Can we travail for a drowning child; but not for a perishing soul? It is not hard to weep when we realize that our little one is sinking below the surface for the last time. Anguish is spontaneous then. Not hard to agonize when we see the casket containing all that we love on earth being borne out of the home. Ah, no; tears are natural at such a time! But oh, to realize and know that souls, precious, never dying souls are perishing all around us, going out into the blackness of darkness and despair, eternally lost, and yet to feel no anguish, shed no tears, know no travail! How cold our hearts are! How little we know of the compassion of Jesus! And yet God can give us this, and the fault is ours if we do not have it.

Jacob, you remember, travailed until he prevailed. But oh, who is doing it today? Who is really travailing in prayer? How many, even of our most spiritual Christian leaders are content to spend half an hour a day on their knees, and then pride themselves on the time they have given to God! We expect extraordinary results, and extraordinary results are quite possible; signs and wonders will follow, but only through extraordinary efforts in the spiritual realm. Hence, nothing short of continuous, agonizing pleading for souls, hours upon hours, days and nights of prayer will ever avail. Therefore, "gird yourselves, and lament ye priests; howl, ye ministers of the altar: come, lie all night in sackcloth, ye ministers of my God. Sanctify ye a fast, call a solemn assembly, gather the elders and all the inhabitants of the land unto the house of the Lord your God, and cry unto the Lord." (Joel 1: 13-14.) Oh yes! Joel knew the secret. Let us then lay aside everything else, and "cry unto the Lord."

"We read in the biographies of our forefathers, who were most successful in winning souls, that they prayed for hours in private. The question therefore arises, can we get the same results without following their example? If we can, then let us prove to the world that we have found a better way; but if not, then in God's name let us begin to follow those who through faith and patience obtained the promise. Our forefathers wept and prayed and agonized before the Lord for sinners to be saved, and would not rest until they were slain by the Sword of the Word of God. That was the secret of their mighty success; when things were slack and would not move they wrestled in prayer till God poured out His Spirit upon the people and sinners were converted." (For Those Who Seek.)

All men of God have become men mighty in prayer. The sun never rose on China, we are told, without finding

Hudson Taylor on his knees. No wonder the China Inland Mission has been so wonderfully owned of God!

Conversion is the operation of the Holy Spirit, and prayer is the power that secures that operation. Souls are not saved by man but by God, and since He works in answer to prayer we have no choice but to follow the Divine plan. Prayer moves the Arm that moves the world.

Prevailing prayer is not easy. Only those who have wrestled with the powers of darkness know how hard it is. Paul says that "we wrestle not against flesh and blood, but against principalities, against powers, against the rulers of the darkness of this world, against spiritual wickedness in high places." (Eph. 6:12.) And when the Holy Spirit prays it is "with groanings which cannot be uttered." (Rom. 8: 26.)

Oh, how few find time for prayer! There is time for everything else, time to sleep and time to eat, time to read the newspaper and the novel, time to visit friends, time for everything else under the sun, but--no time for prayer, the most important of all things, the one great essential.

Think of Susannah Wesley who, in spite of the fact that she had nineteen children, found time to shut herself in her room for a full hour each day, alone with God. My friends, it is not so much a case of finding time as it is of making time. And we can make time if we will.

So important did the Apostles consider it that they would not even wait on tables, but said: "We will give ourselves continually to prayer and to the ministry of the Word." (Acts 6:4.) Yet how many ministers are burdened with the financial side of the work, and how many officials expect them to bear it! No wonder their spiritual work is of such little account !

"And it came to pass in those days, that He went out into a mountain to pray and continued all night in prayer to God." (Luke 6:12.) Such is the record concerning the Son of God; and if it was necessary for Him how much more so for us! Oh, think of it!--"all night in prayer." How many times could that be written of us? Hence, His strength! Hence, our weakness!

How fervently do the prophets of old urge a life of prayer! Hear Isaiah as he exclaims: "Ye that make mention of the Lord, keep not silence, and give Him no rest, till He establish, and till He make Jerusalem a praise in the earth." (Isa. 62:6-7.)

"Let the priests, the ministers of the Lord, weep between the porch and the altar, and let them say, spare Thy people, O Lord, and give not Thine heritage to reproach, that the heathen should rule over them; wherefore should they say among the people, 'Where is their God?' (Joel 2:15.)

And not only did they urge prayer, but they themselves prayed. Daniel says, "I set my face unto the Lord God, to seek by prayer and supplication, with fasting, and sackcloth, and ashes; and I prayed unto the Lord my God, and made my confession." (Dan. 9:3-4.) And Ezra also wielded the same mighty weapon in every time of difficulty. "I fell upon my knees," he says, "and spread out my hands unto the Lord my God." (Ezra 9:5.) Then follows his most remarkable prayer. The same method was followed by Nehemiah. "And it came to pass when I heard their words," he relates, "that I sat down and wept, and mourned certain days and fasted, and prayed before the God of Heaven." (Neh.1:4.)

Such was also the practice of the Early Church. When Peter was in prison it is stated that "prayer was made without ceasing of the Church unto God for him," and "many were gathered together praying."

And now in closing may we turn to the record of God's dealings with His honored servants, and hear what they have to say about the secret of results. And oh, may He put upon us the burden of prayer and supplication that rested upon these mighty spiritual giants and filled them with such travail!

"John Livingstone spent the whole night prior to June 21, 1630, in prayer and conference, being designated to preach next day. After he had been speaking for an hour and a half a few drops of rain disconcerted the people, but Livingstone asking them if they had any shelter from the storm of God's wrath went on another hour. There were about 500 converted on the spot."--Livingstone of Shotts.

"I once knew a minister who had a Revival fourteen winters in succession. I did not know how to account for it, till I saw one of his members get up in a prayer meeting and make a confession. 'Brethren,' said he, 'I have been long in the habit of praying every Saturday night till after midnight, for the descent of the Holy Ghost upon us. And now, brethren,' and he began to weep, 'I confess that I have neglected it for two or three weeks.' The secret was out. That minister had a praying church."--Chas. G. Finney.

"Prevailing, or effectual prayer is that prayer which attains the blessing that it seeks. It is that prayer which effectually moves God. The very idea of effectual prayer is that it effects its object."-Chas. G. Finney.

"In a certain town there had been no Revival for many years; the Church was nearly extinct, the youth were all unconverted and desolation reigned unbroken. There lived in a retired part of the town an aged man, a blacksmith by trade, and of so stammering a tongue that it was painful to hear him speak. On one Friday, as he was at work in his shop alone, his mind became greatly exercised about the state of the Church and of the impenitent. His agony became so great that he was induced to lay by his work, lock the shop door, and spend the afternoon in prayer.

"He prevailed, and on the Sabbath called on the minister and desired him to appoint a 'conference meeting.' After some hesitation, the minister consented, observing however, that he feared few would attend. He appointed it the same evening at a large private house. When evening came more assembled than could be accommodated in the house. All were silent for a time, until one sinner broke out in tears, and said if anyone could pray, would they pray for him. Another followed, and another, and still another, until it was found that persons from every quarter of the town were under deep conviction. And what was remarkable was that they all dated their conviction at the hour the old man was praying in his shop. A powerful Revival followed. Thus this old stammering man prevailed, and as a prince had power with God."-Char. G. Finney.

"'I have pleaded with God this day for hours, in the wood, for souls: He will give them. I know His sign. I shall have souls tonight. Yours, I trust, will be one.' Night came, and with it such a power as I had never felt. Cries for mercy rang all over the chapel. Before the sermon was done, I, with many others, fell upon my knees to implore salvation."--One of Thos. Collins' Converts.

"I went to my lonely retreat among the rocks. I wept much as I besought the Lord to give me souls."--Thos. Collins.

"I spent Friday in secret fasting, meditation, and prayer for help on the Lord's Day. About the middle of the sermon a man cried out; at the cry my soul ran over. I fell to prayer, nor could we preach any more for cries and tears all over the chapel. We continued in intercessions, and salvation came." --Thos. Collins.

"He gave himself unto prayer. Woods and lonely wayside places became closets. In such exercises time flew unheeded. He stopped amid the solitary crags to pray, and Heaven so met him there that hours elapsed unconsciously. Strong in the might of such baptisms, he became bold to declare the cross, and willing to bear it."--Life of Thos. Collins.

"It loaded me down with great agony. As I returned to my room I felt almost as if I should stagger under the burden that was on my mind; and I struggled, and groaned, and agonized, but could not frame to present the case before God in words, but only in groans and tears. The Spirit struggled within me with groanings that could not be uttered."--Chas. G. Finney.

"I proposed that we should observe a closet concert of prayer for the revival of God's work; that we should pray at sunrise, at noon, and at sunset, in our closets, and continue this for one week, when we should come together again and see what further was to be done. No other means were used for the revival of God's work. But the spirit of prayer was immediately poured out wonderfully upon the young converts. Before the week was out I learned that some of them, when they would attempt to observe this season of prayer, would lose all their strength and be unable to rise to their feet or even stand upon their knees in their closets; and that some would be prostrate on the floor, and pray with unutterable groanings for the Outpouring of the Spirit of God. The Spirit was poured out and before the week ended all the meetings were thronged; and there was as much interest in religion, I think, as there has been at any time during the Revival."--Chas. G. Finney.

"I have often seen him come down stairs in the morning after spending several hours in prayer, with his eyes swollen with weeping. He would soon introduce the subject of his anxiety by saying, 'I am a broken hearted man; yes, indeed, I am an unhappy man; not for myself, but on account of others. God has given me such a sight of the value of precious souls that I cannot live if souls are not saved. Oh, give me souls, or else I die!' "--Life of John Smith.

"God enabled me to so agonize in prayer that I was quite wet with perspiration, though in the shade and the cool wind. My soul was drawn out very much from the world, for multitudes of souls."--David Brainerd.

"Near the middle of the afternoon God enabled me to wrestle ardently in intercession for my friends. But just at night the Lord visited me marvelously in prayer. I think my soul never was in such an agony before. I felt no restraint; for the treasures of Divine grace were opened to me. I wrestled for my friends, for the ingathering of souls, for multitudes of poor souls, and for many that I thought were the children of God, personally in many different places. I was in such an agony from sun, half an hour high, till near dark, that I was all over wet with sweat.--David Brainerd.

"I withdrew from prayer, hoping for strength from above. In prayer I was exceedingly enlarged and my soul was as much drawn out as I ever remember it to have been in my life. I was in such anguish, and pleaded with so much earnestness and importunity, that when I rose from my knees I felt extremely weak and overcome I could scarcely walk straight; my joints were loosed; the sweat ran down my face and body; and nature seemed as if it would dissolve."--David Brainerd.

"Prayer must carry on our work, as well as preaching. He does not preach heartily to his people who does not pray for them. If we do not prevail with God to give them repentance and faith, we are not likely to prevail with them to repent and believe. Paul gives us frequently his example of praying night and day for his hearers."--Richard Baxter.

"Several members of Jonathan Edwards' church had spent the whole night in prayer before he preached his memorable sermon, 'Sinners in the Hands of an Angry God.' The Holy Ghost was so mightily poured out, and

God so manifest in holiness and majesty during the preaching of that sermon, that the elders threw their arms around the pillars of the church and cried, 'Lord, save us, we are slipping down to hell!'"

"Almost every night there has been a shaking among the people; and I have seen nearly twenty set at liberty. I believe I should have seen many more, but I cannot yet find one pleading man. There are many good people; but I have found no wrestlers with God. At two or three small places, we had cries for mercy; and several were left in a state of deep distress."--Wm. Bramwell.

"Where the result which he desired did not attend his own ministry, he would spend days and nights almost constantly on his knees, weeping and pleading before God; and especially deploring his own inadequacy to the great work of saving souls. He was at times when he perceived no movement in the church, literally in agonies; travailing in birth for precious souls, till he saw Christ magnified in their salvation."--Life of John Smith.

"If you spend several hours in prayer daily, you will see great things."--John Nelson. "He made it a rule to rise out of bed about twelve o'clock, and sit up till two, for prayer and converse with God; then he slept till four; at which time he always rose."--Life of John Nelson.

"Be instant and constant in prayer. Study, books, eloquence, fine sermons, are all nothing without prayer. Prayer brings the spirit, the life, the power."--Memoir of David Stoner.

"I find it necessary to begin at five in the morning and to pray at all opportunities till ten, or eleven at night."-- Wm. Bramwell.

But must we go back to these mighty men of old? Are there not some today who will ask God to burden them? May we not even in this generation have a Revival in answer to faithful, believing, travailing, prevailing prayer? Oh, then, "Lord, teach us not how to pray, but to pray."

CHAPTER IV THE ENDUEMENT OF POWER

The Holy Spirit is able to make the Word as successful now as in the days of the apostles. He can bring in souls by hundreds and thousands as well as by ones and twos. The reason why we are no more prosperous is that we have not the Holy Spirit with us in might and power as in early times.

"If we had the Spirit sealing our ministry with power it would signify very little about talent. Men might be poor and uneducated, their words might be broken and ungrammatical; but if the might of the Spirit attended them, the humblest evangelist would be more successful than the most learned of divines, or the most eloquent of preachers.

"It is extraordinary power from God, not talent, that wins the day. It is extraordinary spiritual unction not extraordinary mental power, that we need. Mental power may fill a chapel but spiritual power fills the church with soul anguish. Mental power may gather a large congregation. but only spiritual power will save souls. What we need is spiritual power."--Chas. H. Spurgeon.

"Let the Spirit be lacking, and there may be wisdom of words, but not the wisdom of God; the powers of oratory, but not the power of God; the demonstration of argument and the logic of the schools, but not the demonstration of the Holy Spirit, the all-convincing logic of His lightning flash, such as convinced Saul before the Damascus gate. When the Spirit was outpoured the disciples were all filled with power from on high, the most unlettered tongue could silence gainsayers, and with its new fire burn its way through obstacles as flames fanned by mighty winds sweep through forests."-Arthur T. Pierson.

"The ministers of the Gospel must needs have this power of the Holy Spirit, because otherwise they are not sufficient for the ministry. For no man is sufficient for the work of the ministry by any natural parts and abilities of his own, nor yet by any acquired parts of human learning and knowledge, but only by this power of the Holy Spirit; till he be endued with this, notwithstanding all his other accomplishments, he is altogether insufficient. And therefore the very apostles were to keep silent, till they were endued with this power; they were to wait at Jerusalem, till they had received the promise of the Spirit, and not to preach till then."

"If they have not this power of the Holy Spirit they have not power at all. And therefore, seeing the ministers of the Gospel have not power from beneath, they must needs have power from on high; seeing they have no fleshly power, they must needs have spiritual power; seeing they have no power from earth and from men, they must needs have power from heaven and from God: that is, the power of the Holy Spirit coming on them; or else they have no power at all."--Wm. Dell.

But who is in the Anointing today? Who has the experience? It is promised; it is indispensible, and yet we labor on without it, working in the flesh like the disciples who toiled all night and caught nothing. And just so will it be with us. An hour's work in the Spirit will accomplish more than a year's work in the flesh. And the Fruit will

36

remain. "It is the Spirit that quickeneth; the flesh profiteth nothing." (Jno. 6:63.) "That which is born of the flesh is flesh, and that which is born of the Spirit is Spirit." (Jno. 3:6.) It is Holy Spirit Fruit we want, pure gold without alloy, and nothing less. Not the kind that comes undone, but the genuine article that stands the test of time and Eternity; the kind we find at the prayer meeting as well as the Sunday services. Is this the kind of Fruit we are bearing? Is there conviction, and do souls come through into the glorious liberty of the children of God?

But have we the Enduement of Power? I don't mean have we "claimed it" and gone forth reckoning it ours, but, have we the experience? If there is no Outcome, we certainly have not. If we are Spirit-filled there will be Holy Spirit Fruit. Men will break down in our meetings and sob out their sins to God. Let us see the Fruit if we are to believe in the Anointing. "Ye shall receive Power." And when Peter got it, 3,000 were saved. And so with John Smith, Samuel Morris, Chas. G. Finney and others-- there was Fruit. This is the evidence, this is the test, and only this. If I am a man of God endued with power from on High souls will break down under my preaching; if I am not, nothing out of the ordinary will take place. Let this be the test for every preacher. By this we stand or fall.

"I was powerfully converted on the morning of the 10th of October, 1821," writes Chas. G. Finney. "In the evening of the same day I received overwhelming baptisms of the Holy Ghost, that went through me, as it seemed to me, body and soul. 1 immediately found myself endued with such power from on high that a few words dropped here and there to individuals were the means of their immediate conversion. My words seemed to fasten like barbed arrows in the souls of men. They cut like a sword. They broke the heart like a hammer. Multitudes can attest to this. Oftentimes a word dropped without my remembering it would fasten conviction, and often result in almost immediate conversion. Sometimes I would find myself, in a great measure, empty of this power. I would go and visit, and find that I made no saving impression. I would exhort and pray, with the same result. I would then set apart a day for private fasting and prayer, fearing that this power had departed from me, and would inquire anxiously after the reason of this apparent emptiness. After humbling myself, and crying out for help, the power would return upon me with all its freshness. This has been the experience of my life.

"This power is a great marvel. I have many times seen people unable to endure the Word. The most simple and ordinary statements would cut men off their seats like a sword, would take away their strength, and render them almost helpless as dead men. Several times it has been true in my experience that I could not raise my voice, or say anything in prayer or exhortation, except in the mildest manner, without overcoming them. This power seems sometimes to pervade the atmosphere of the one who is highly charged with it. Many times great numbers of persons in a community will be clothed with this power when the very atmosphere of the whole place seems to be charged with the life of God. Strangers coming into it, and passing through the place will be instantly smitten with conviction of sin and in many instances converted to Christ. When Christians humble themselves and consecrate their all afresh to Christ, and ask for this power, they will often receive such a baptism that they will be instrumental in converting more souls in one day than in all their lifetime before. While Christians remain humble enough to retain this power, the work of conversion will go on, till whole communities and regions of country are converted to Christ. The same is true of the ministry."

Where is the soul anguish of by-gone days, the wounded conscience, the sleepless nights, the groans and cries, the awful conviction of sin, the sobs and tears of the lost? Would to God we might hear and see it in this generation!

And who is to blame, the people? Do we attribute it to their hardness of heart? Does the fault lie there? Oh, no, my brethren, the fault is ours; we are to blame. Were we what and where we ought to be, the signs would still follow as in the days of old. Then should not every failure, every sermon that fails to break the people down, drive us to our knees and result in deep heart searching, and humiliation. Let us never blame the people. If our churches are cold and unresponsive, it is because we are cold. Like pastor like people.

Oh how many there are who have been robbed of their testimony or who have never known the power of the Holy Spirit in their work! Their service is ineffective and their witness bearing null and void, while they accomplish little or nothing for God. Oh, yes, they go through the motions and sometimes they are very active, but it is all in the energy of the flesh, and no spiritual results follow. Souls are not saved nor are believers edified and built up in the Faith. Their preaching produces no Fruit and their Ministry is a ghastly failure. Oh, what a disappointing experience!

But, thank God, this need not be, for "Ye shall receive power," is His promise, and, "Tarry ye until ye be endued with power from on High," His command.

The passage in Acts 1:8 literally reads: "Ye shall receive the power of the Holy Spirit coming upon you," so that the Anointing or Enduement of Power is that experience which is the result produced by the Holy Spirit coming upon the believer and equipping him for service.

Such Anointings are only received in the soul-agonies of deep travailing prayer. The nights and days of agonizing prayer for the souls of men, the countless hours of intercession that we find in the life of David Brainerd, the mighty wrestlings with the spiritual powers of darkness until the body is wet with perspiration that were so common to John Smith--this is something that goes much further than present-day teaching, but it is the only thing that will produce the Fruit, and do the work of which we are speaking.

It is from these hours of prevailing prayer that we go forth to our work in the Anointing to wield the Sword of the Spirit with deadly effect. Prayer is the secret. There can be no substitute. And for each special work there must be a special Anointing. It is not merely a matter of yielding and believing now. Ah, no! The glorious supernatural results that I am talking of are not obtained so easily. It costs and costs tremendously.

"'They continued with one accord in prayer and supplication.' Prayer earnest, prayer united, and prayer

40

persevering, these are the conditions; and, these being fulfilled, we shall assuredly be 'endued with Power from on High.' We should never expect that the Power will fall upon us just because we happen once to awake and ask for it. Nor have any community of Christians a right to look for a great Manifestation of the Spirit, if they are not all ready to join in supplication, and 'with one accord,' to wait and pray as if it were the concern of each one.

"It is only by waiting before that throne of grace that we become endued with the Holy Fire; but he who waits there long and believingly will imbibe that Fire, and come forth from his communion with God, bearing tokens of where he has been. For the individual believer, and, above all, for every labourer in the Lord's vineyard, the only way to gain spiritual Power is by secret waiting at the throne of God, for the Baptism.

"If thou, then, wouldst have thy soul surcharged with the Fire of God, so that those who come nigh to thee shall feel some mysterious influence proceeding out from thee, thou must draw nigh to the source of that Fire, to the throne of God and of the Lamb, and shut thyself out from the world--that cold world, which so swiftly steals our Fire away. Enter into thy closet, and shut to thy door, and there, isolated, before the throne, await the Baptism; then the Fire shall fill thee, and when thou comest forth, holy Power will attend thee, and thou shalt labour not in thine own strength, but 'in demonstration of the Spirit, and of Power.' "--Wm. Arthur.

There are many in a false experience who think they are in the Anointing when they are not. All I can say is that the evidence, the proof is lacking. If they were there would be the same things happen that those who were truly Anointed always witnessed. If all the professed Baptisms and Fillings of the Holy Spirit in the modern conventions were real the whole country would be on fire. Nay, if just one man or one woman received the Anointing, the towns and villages for miles around might be swept by a mighty Revival, and thousands brought under deep conviction of sin and made to cry for mercy. The proof of the Anointing is the Outcome. The evidence that the spirit of Elijah had fallen on Elisha was the fact that he, too, smote the waters of Jordan and they divided.

"Why is it so hard to get?" you ask. Why? Because God will not pour His Spirit on the flesh. He must do His work in us first, and generally it takes a long time, for we will not let Him have his way with us. The saviour of our own name, love of praise, or some such sinful obstacle blocks Him at every turn. He cannot humble us; He is unable to break our hearts because we will not yield.

Or else, because He cannot trust us with so great an honor. He knows we will only make shipwreck of it. Oh, the sad, heart-rending incidents of men and women who were once used in mighty Revivals, and in the Anointing of the Spirit brought hundreds of souls to God, who lost that cherished blessing and worked in the flesh ever after, accomplishing little or nothing! They counted it too lightly; they became puffed up and proud; they allowed some little sin to come in; the Holy Spirit was grieved away. and they found themselves, like Samson of old, shorn of their strength. At one time when they preached souls cried aloud for mercy under awful conviction. Now they beg and coax; the meetings are dead and cold, while

42

only a handful respond, and even these are not Holy Spirit Fruit.

It remains only to insert the testimonies of some who have received the Enduement of Power to convince us of the reality of the experience. And if God could give it to one or a dozen He can give it to all.

"For thirteen years," writes Evan Roberts, "I had prayed for the Spirit; and this is the way I was led to pray. William Davies, the deacon, said one night in the society: 'Remember to be faithful. What if the Spirit descended and you were absent? Remember Thomas! What a loss he had!'

"I said to myself: 'I will have the Spirit;' and through every kind of weather and in spite of all difficulties, I went to the meetings. Many times, on seeing other boys with the boats on the tide, I was tempted to turn back and join them. But, no. I said to myself: 'Remember your resolve,' and on I went. I went faithfully to the meetings for prayer throughout the ten or eleven years I prayed for a Revival. It was the Spirit that moved me thus to think."

At a certain morning meeting which Evan Roberts attended, the evangelist in one of his petitions besought that the Lord would "bend us." The Spirit seemed to say to Roberts: "That's what you need, to be bent." And thus he describes his experience: "I felt a living force coming into my bosom. This grew and grew, and I was almost bursting. My bosom was boiling. What boiled in me was that verse: 'God commending His love.' I fell on my knees with my arms over the seat in front of me; the tears and perspiration flowed freely. I thought blood was gushing forth." Certain friends approached to wipe his face.

Meanwhile he was crying out, "O Lord, bend me! Bend me!" Then suddenly the glory broke.

Mr. Roberts adds: "After I was bent, a wave of peace came over me, and the audience sang, 'I hear Thy welcome voice.' And as they sang I thought about the bending at the Judgment Day, and I was filled with compassion for those that would have to bend on that day, and I wept.

"Henceforth, the salvation of souls became the burden of my heart. From that time I was on fire with a desire to go through all Wales, and if it were possible, I was willing to pay God for the privilege of going."

Such was the experience of Evan Roberts, God's honored instrument in the great Welsh Revival. Now let us listen to the testimonies of John Wesley and Christmas Evans:

"About three in the morning as we were continuing instant in prayer, the power of God came mightily upon us, insomuch that many cried out for exceeding joy, and many fell to the ground. As soon as we recovered a little from the awe and amazement at the presence of His Majesty, we broke out with one voice, 'We praise Thee, O God, we acknowledge Thee to be the Lord.' "--John Wesley.

"I was weary of a cold heart towards Christ and His sacrifice, and the work of His Spirit---of a cold heart in the pulpit, in secret prayer, and in study, for fifteen years previously, I had felt my heart burning within, as if going to Emmaus with Jesus.

"On a day ever to be remembered by me, as I was climbing up towards Cadair Idris, I considered it to be incumbent upon me to pray, however hard I felt in my heart, and however worldly the frame of my spirit was. Having begun in the name of Jesus, I soon felt, as it were, the fetters loosening, and the old hardness of heart softening, and, as I thought, mountains of frost and snow dissolving and melting within me.

"This engendered confidence in my soul in the promise of the Holy Ghost. I felt my whole mind relieved from some great bondage; tears flowed copiously, and I was constrained to cry out for the gracious visits of God, by restoring to my soul the joys of His salvation; and that He would visit the churches of the saints, and nearly all the ministers in the principality by their names.

"This struggle lasted for three hours: it rose again and again, like one wave after another, or a high flowing tide, driven by a strong wind, until my nature became faint by weeping and crying. Thus I resigned myself to Christ, body and soul, gifts and labors--all my life---every day, and every hour that remained for me; and all my cares I committed to Christ.

"From this time I was made to expect the goodness of God to churches, and to myself. In the first religious meetings after this, I felt as if I had been removed from the cold and sterile regions of spiritual frost, into the verdant fields of Divine promises. The former striving with God in prayer, and the longing anxiety for the conversion of sinners, which I experienced at Leyn, were now restored. I had a hold of the promises of God.

"The result was, when I returned home, the first thing that arrested my attention was that the Spirit was working also in the brethren in Anglesea, inducing in them a spirit of prayer, especially in two of the deacons,

45

who were particularly importunate that God would visit us in mercy, and render the Word of His grace effectual amongst us for the conversion of sinners."

Now, apparently strengthened as by a new spirit, with "might in the inner man," he labored with renewed energy and zeal; and new and singular blessings descended upon his labors. In two years, his ten preaching places in Anglesea were increased to twenty, and six hundred converts were added to the church under his immediate care.--Christmas Evans.

UNCTION

Oh, for the Spirit's mighty pow'r,

The Unction from above!

Oh, for a gracious heav'nly show'r,

The fulness of God's love!

This, only this, our one great need--

Naught else can e'er prevail;

Thus for the Unction now we plead--

It only can avail.

Our sins to God we now confess;

To Him we yield our all,

Believing He will surely bless

As on His name we call.

And so we give ourselves to pray'r

That God may make us meet;

For He must first our hearts prepare--

His work in us complete.

Then shall men turn to Calv'ry's stream

With burdened hearts of woe;

Salvation then shall be our theme,

And earth be heav'n below.

CHAPTER V CONVICTION

THERE is one thing that was always prominent in the great Revivals of past days, viz., a deep and a true conviction of sin. And it is one of the vital elements that is lacking today.

How disappointing are the methods of present-day Evangelism! How shallow and unreal when compared with the genuine work of the Spirit! All this pressing, coaxing, urging; standing up, raising the hand, coming to the front, etc., all such public display as it is carried on in modern campaigns, is surely not the work of the Holy Spirit.

Not that pleading with men is unscriptural. God forbid! But with conviction absent it is fruitless. And modern Evangelism with its chilling irreverence, uncalled for slang, and spirit-grieving frivolity, let alone its lamentable professionalism, can by no means lead up to conviction of sin and result in a spiritual outcome.

Where there is genuine conviction of sin it is not necessary to urge, coax or press in the energy of the flesh; sinners will come without being asked; they will come because they must. Those who go home from the meeting unable to eat or sleep because of deep conviction do not need to be coaxed and urged to seek relief.

In the modern campaign the evangelist calls upon people to accept Christ, and rightly so. But oh, that we could hear sinners calling upon Christ to accept them! People take salvation today in such a cold, formal, matter-of-fact, business-like sort of way, that it appears as though they are doing God an honor in condescending to receive His offer of Redemption. Their eyes are dry, their sense of sin absent; nor is there any sign of penitence and contrition. They look upon it as a manly thing to do. But oh, if there were conviction! if they came with hearts bowed down, yea! broken and contrite, came with the cry of the guilt-laden soul "God be merciful to me a sinner!"--came trembling with the burning life and death question of the Philippian jailor: "What must I do to be saved?"--what converts they would be!

But in our Twentieth Century Evangelism such is not the case. Men are urged to be saved before they know they are lost, to believe without being convicted of their need. The fruit is picked before it is ripe, and of course the work is bound to come undone. If we are to get Holy Spirit Fruit, God must prepare the ground, the Holy Spirit must convict of sin before men can truly believe. It is right to tell people to believe when God has done His work in their hearts, but first they must feel their need.

Let us wait until the Spirit of God has done His part before we say: "Believe on the Lord Jesus Christ and thou shalt be saved." Let us first see the signs of conviction as in the case of the Philippian jailor. And when their anguish is so deep that they are forced to cry aloud: "What must I do to be saved?" then we will know that they are ready to be exhorted to trust and exercise faith in Christ, but not until then.

"There is another Gospel, too popular in the present day, which seems to exclude conviction of sin and repentance from the scheme of Salvation; which demands from the sinner a mere intellectual assent to the fact of his guilt and sinfulness, and a like intellectual assent to the fact and sufficiency of Christ's atonement; and such assent yielded, tells him to go in peace, and to he happy in the assurance that the Lord Jesus has made all right between his soul and God; thus crying peace, peace, when there is no peace.

"Flimsy and false conversions of this sort may be one reason why so many who assume the Christian profession dishonor God and bring reproach on the church by their inconsistent lives, and by their ultimate relapse into worldliness and sin. The whole counsel of God must be declared. 'By the law is the knowledge of sin.' Sin must be felt before it can be mourned. Sinners must sorrow before they can be comforted. True conversions are the great want of the times. Conversions such as were common once, and shall be again, when the church shakes off her lethargy, takes hold upon God's strength, and brings down the ancient power. Then, as of old, sinners will quail before the terror of the Lord."--J. H. Lord.

Would we think of calling a doctor before we were sick? Do we urge people who are well and strong to hasten to the physician? Does the man who is swimming well beseech those on the shore to come and save him? Certainly not! But let sickness come, and at once we feel our need and a doctor is called. We know that we require a remedy. When we feel ourselves sinking below the surface, and realize that we are drowning, we will then soon call for help, and oh, the agony through which we pass as we find ourselves going down and know that unless some one saves us, we are lost and must perish!

So it is with a perishing soul. When a man is convicted of his lost condition he will cry out in the bitter anguish of his heart: "What must I do to be saved?" He will need no urging, no coaxing; it is a matter of life or death to him, and he will do anything to be saved.

So you see I am not talking about an Evangelistic campaign. That is frequently man's work, and sometimes entirely so. But this Revival--oh, the glory of it! all, all of God! Man has no room for honor here. While these special evangelistic services--how different they are! Great excitement, much outward joy, scores of reported converts, and then--a spurious outcome, a false state. This "accepting Christ" theory without conviction, a head belief, but no New Birth, no "Born Again" experience--what a mockery it is!

It is this lack of conviction that results in a spurious Revival, and causes the work to come undone. It is one thing to hold up the hand and sign a decision card, but it is quite another thing to get saved. Souls must be brought into clear and abiding liberty if the work is to last. It is one thing to have hundreds of professed converts during the excitement of the campaign, but it is another thing to come back five years after and find them still there.

John Bunyan understood it well when he pictured Christian with his great load of sin on his back, and described his exercise of soul until he got rid of his burden at the foot of the Cross.

God has placed His own value on His word. He calls it a "Fire," a "Hammer" and a "Sword." Now fire burns; a blow from a hammer hurts; while a cut from a sword causes real pain. And when His Word is proclaimed in the power of the Anointing it will have exactly the same results. It will burn like a fire, break like a hammer and pierce like a sword, and the spiritual or mental pain will be just as severe and real as the physical. And if not,--then there is something wrong either with the messenger or the message.

"Were a person who had committed an awful crime to be suddenly arrested; were his guilt brought home to his conscience by some messenger of justice, in the pointed language of Holy Writ, 'Thou art the man;' it would be perfectly natural for the culprit to turn pale, to falter in his speech, to tremble, and to present every symptom of real agony and distress. When Belshazzar, the proud Assyrian monarch, saw the appearance of a man's hand writing upon the plaster of the wall of his palace, his countenance was changed, and his thoughts troubled him, so that the joints of his loins were loosed and his knees smote one against another. And the effects have never yet been deemed unnatural. Why then should it be thought strange to behold sinners who have been powerfully awakened by the Spirit of God, who are so deeply convinced of the enormity of their crimes as to apprehend they are every moment in danger of dropping into the burning lake, who imagine that hell is moved from beneath to meet them at their coming, why should it be thought unnatural for such persons to discover outward symptoms of the alarming distress and agitation felt within?" -- Memoir of Wm. Bramwell.

Such has been the experience of God's servants all down the centuries. In every Revival there has been deep conviction of sin. Some of the records sound strange indeed to those who have known and studied nothing but Twentieth Century Evangelism. Incidents such as the following were common to these men.

"About the middle of the sermon a man cried out. I fell to prayer, nor could we preach any more for cries and tears all over the chapel."--Thos. Collins.

"Cries for mercy rang all over the chapel. Before the sermon was done, I with many others, fell upon my knees to implore Salvation."--One of Thos. Collins' Converts.

"The sermon was swallowed up in victory. Seekers left their pews, and trooping, unbidden, up the aisles, knelt around the communion rail." -- Thos. Collins.

"A Quaker who stood by was not a little displeased at the dissimulation of these creatures, and was biting his lips and knitting his brows, when he dropped down as thunder-struck. The agony he was in was even terrible to behold. We besought God not to lay folly to his charge, and he soon lifted up his head and cried aloud, 'Now I know thou art a prophet of the Lord.' " --John Wesley.

"J. H. was a man of regular life and conversation, one that constantly attended public prayers and sacrament, and was zealous for the church, and against dissenters of every denomination. Being informed that people fell into strange fits at the societies, he came to see and judge for himself. But he was less satisfied than before; inasmuch, that he went about to see his acquaintances one after another till one o'clock in the morning, and labored above measure to convince them it was a delusion of the devil.

"We were going home when one met us in the street, and informed us that J. H. was fallen raving mad.

"It seems he sat down to dinner, but had in mind first to end the sermon he had borrowed on Salvation by Faith. In reading the last page, he changed colour, fell off his chair and began screaming terribly, and beating himself against the ground.

"The neighbors were alarmed and flocked together to the house. Between one and two I came in and found him on the floor, the room being full of people whom his wife would have kept without, but he cried out aloud, 'No, let them all come, let all the world see the just judgment of God.' Two or three men were holding him as best they could. He immediately fixed his eyes upon me, and stretching out his hand cried, 'Aye, this is he who I said was a deceiver of the people. But God has overtaken me. I said it was all a delusion. But this is no delusion.' He then roared out, 'O, thou devil! thou cursed devil! yea, thou legion of devils! thou canst not stay. Christ will cast thee out! I know His work is begun. Tear me to pieces if thou wilt, but thou canst not hurt me !' He then beat himself against the ground again, his breast heaving at the same time, as in the pangs of death, and great drops of sweats trickling down his face.

"We all betook ourselves to prayer; his pangs ceased and both his body and soul were set at liberty."--John Wesley.

"The power of God was present. They came to be saved, and were not disappointed. The sobs and cries were wonderful. It seemed as if God had come down in terror and power; as if the Spirit were passing through every region of every soul, diffusing Himself through all its capacities, and recesses; throwing light into the understanding, assailing and subverting the fortress of sin in the heart; revealing Himself as the antagonist of sin--disturbing and tracking it in all its windings--stirring the soul to its depths, drawing it slowly, but surely, to a crisis--piling up these sentences of condemnation, one upon another, until the whole soul, collecting all its energies into one out-cry for mercy, exclaimed, 'God, be merciful to me a sinner, what must I do to be saved? Save, Lord, or I perish! O, save or I sink into hell. Heal my soul for I have sinned against Thee!"--James Caughey.

"The power of God seemed to descend upon the assembly like a mighty, rushing wind, and with an astonishing energy bore down all before it. I stood amazed at the influence, which seized the audience almost universally; and could compare it to nothing more apt than the irresistible force of a mighty torrent or a swelling deluge that with its insupportable weight and pressure bears down and sweeps before it whatever comes in its way. Almost all persons of all ages were bowed down with concern together, and scarcely one was able to withstand the shock of this surprising operation; old men and women, who had been drunken wretches for many years and some little children, not more than six or seven years of age, appeared in distress for their souls, as well as persons of middle age.

"The most stubborn hearts were now obliged to bow. A principal man among the Indians, who, before, was most secure and self-righteous, and thought his state good, because he knew more than the generality of the Indians had formerly done, and who with a great degree of confidence the day before told me he had been a Christian more than ten years, was now brought under solemn concern for his soul and wept bitterly. Another man advanced in years, who had been a murderer, a conjurer, and a notorious drunkard, was likewise brought now to cry for mercy with many tears, and to complain much that he could be no more concerned when he saw his dangers so very great.

"They were almost universally praying and crying for mercy in every part of the house, and many out of doors, and numbers could neither go nor stand. Their concern was so great, each one for himself, that none seemed to take any notice of those about them, but each prayed freely for himself."--David Brainerd.

"A young Indian woman, who, I believe, never knew before that she had a soul, nor ever thought of any such thing, hearing that there was something strange among the Indians, came to see what was the matter. On the way to the Indians she called at my lodgings; and, when I told her that I designed presently to preach to the Indians, she laughed and seemed to mock; but went however to them.

"I had not proceeded far in my public discourse before she felt effectually that she had a soul, and before I had concluded my discourse, was so convinced of her sin and misery and so distressed with concern for her soul's salvation that she seemed like one pierced through with a dart, and she cried out incessantly. She could neither go nor stand, nor sit on her seat without being held up.

"After public service was over, she lay flat on the ground praying earnestly, and would take no notice of, nor give any answer to, any who spoke to her. I hearkened to what she said, and perceived the burden of her prayer to be 'Have mercy on me and help me give you my heart.' Thus she continued praying incessantly for hours together."-David Brainerd.

"In the midst of my discourse I saw a powerful looking man fall from his seat. As he sunk he groaned and then cried or shrieked out, that he was sinking to hell. He repeated that several times. Of course this created a great excitement. It broke up my preaching; and so great was his anguish that we spent the rest of our time in praying for him. The next morning I inquired for him; and found that he had spent a sleepless night in great anguish of mind."--Chas. G. Finney.

"The chapel was crowded to excess. The Word was 'quick and powerful,' numbers 'were pricked in their hearts,' and in the agony of conviction cried mightily for mercy. The sermon was followed by a prayer meeting. Midnight arrived and the penitents were still upon their knees, resolved to plead till they prevailed. As one and another found peace through believing and withdrew, others whose hearts were stricken filled their places. So intense was the Awakening, that though the squire had retired, the alarmed and sorrowing people could not be induced to leave the chapel, but all night through, and all through the following day and night, the prayer meeting continued without intermission. It was supposed that over one hundred persons were converted, whilst many an old professor received quickening and gave himself to God by a fuller consecration."--Memoir of Squire Brooke.

"Had the preacher fired upon the people with grapeshot, the wounded had not been more numerous, or the cry of anguish more bitter. It was simply impossible to proceed with the discourse. Leaving the pulpit the Squire came down amongst the people to gather the praying men for intercession, whilst he conversed with penitents and endeavoured to assist them into the kingdom."-Memoir of Squire Brooke.

"While engaged in prayer, two of those who came in were awakened and began to cry for mercy.

"No sooner had she communicated the tidings, than her sister was cut to the heart and began to cry for mercy.

"While I was praying, the power of God descended and he and his penitent companion were cut to the heart and wept aloud for their sins.

"While talking with an old woman sixty years of age, she was soon cut to the heart, and in a very short time the Lord set her soul at liberty.

"In visiting from house to house, I fell in with a young woman, to whom I had not spoken many words before she was pricked in the heart and cried for mercy, as one hanging over the pit of hell.

"I had not spoken many words to her before she burst into tears and loud cries. She continued to groan under the weight of her guilty load. The cries and wailings of her broken heart were deeply affecting."--Wm. Carvosso.

"The spirit of the Lord was poured out abundantly and many cried aloud for mercy. Near the close he was like a flame of fire; the people burst into tears on every side, and could say, 'Lo, God is here, of a truth! 'Many cried, yea groaned, aloud for mercy, and God delivered them. Many were deeply convicted and cried out for mercy; an old woman about seventy years of age, was struck in a moment. She fell to the ground, making a frightful noise, and continued speechless and in an agony for above an hour. When she came to herself she jumped off the chair on which she had been placed, clapped her hands, and praised the Lord."--Memoir of Wm. Bramwell.

"I had not discoursed long when the congregation melted into tears. This abated for a few minutes, till a little boy about seven or eight years of age cried out exceeding piteously indeed and wept as though his little heart would break. I asked the little boy what he cried for. He answered 'my sins !' I then asked him what he wanted. He answered, 'Christ!'

"Others were so earnest for a discovery of the Lord to their souls that their eager crying obliged me to stop, and I prayed over them, as I saw their agonies and distress increase. Oh, the distress and anguish of their souls! oh, the pains that were upon them!

"Many of the assembled were deeply affected, groaning and sobbing; there was a great weeping and mourning." --Wm. Bramwell.

"When the conviction as to its mental process reaches its crisis, the person, through weakness, is unable to sit or stand, and either kneels or lies down. A great number of convicted persons in this town and neighborhood, and now I believe in all directions in the north where the Revival prevails, are "smitten down" as suddenly and they fall as nerveless and paralyzed and powerless, as if killed instantly by a shotgun. They fall with a deep groan, some with a wild cry of horror--the greater number with the intensely earnest plea, 'Lord Jesus, have mercy on my soul !' The whole frame trembles like an aspen leaf, an intolerable weight is felt upon the chest, a choking sensation is experienced and relief from this found only in the loud, urgent prayer for deliverance, usually the bodily distress and mental anguish continue till some degree of confidence in Christ is found. Then the look, the tone, the gestures, instantly change. The aspect of anguish and despair is changed for that of gratitude, and triumph, and adoration. The language and the looks, and terrible struggles, and loud desperate depreciation, tell convincingly, as the parties themselves declare, that they are in deadly conflict with the old serpent. The perspiration rolls off the anguished victims; their very hair is moistened. Some pass through this exhausting conflict several times; others but once. There is no appetite for food; many will eat nothing for a number of days. They do not sleep, though they may lie down with their eyes shut."--The Irish Revival 1859.

'The power of the Lord's spirit became so mighty upon their souls as to carry all before it, like the rushing mighty wind of Pentecost. Some were screaming out in agony; others--and among these strong men--fell to the ground as if they had been dead. I was obliged to give out a psalm, our voices being mingled with the mourning and groans of many prisoners sighing for deliverance." --Wm. Burns.

"A revival always includes conviction of sin on the part of the church. Back-slidden professors cannot wake up and begin right away in the service of God without deep

60

searchings of heart. The fountains of sin need to be broken up. In a true Revival, Christians are always brought under such conviction; they see their sins in such a light that often they find it impossible to maintain a hope of their acceptance with God. It does not always go to that extent, but there are always, in a genuine Revival, deep convictions of sin, and often cases of abandoning all hope." --Chas. G. Finney.

CHAPTER VI OBSTACLES

There is only one obstacle that can block up the channel and choke God's power, and that is SIN. Sin is the great barrier. It alone can hinder the work of the Spirit and prevent a Revival. "If I regard iniquity in my heart," declared David, "The Lord will not hear me." (Psalm 66:18.) And in Isaiah 59:12, we have these significant words: "Behold, the Lord's hand is not shortened, that it cannot save; neither his ear heavy, that it cannot hear: but your iniquities have separated between you and your God, and your sins have hid His face from you, that He will not hear." Sin then is the great barrier, and it must be put away. Nor is there any alternative. There can be no compromise. God will not work as long as there is iniquity covered up.

In Hosea 10:12 we read, "Sow to yourselves in righteousness, reap in mercy; break up your fallow ground: for it is time to seek the Lord, till He come and rain righteousness upon you." And in II Chronicles 7:14 the promise of blessing is vouchsafed, based, however, upon unalterable conditions: "If my people, which are called by my name," declares the Lord, "shall humble themselves, and pray, and seek my face, and turn from their wicked ways; then will I hear from heaven, and will forgive their sin, and will heal their land." Hence, nothing short of a broken heart over sin, full confession and restitution will satisfy God. Sin must be forsaken utterly.

And not only sorrow for the consequences and punishment of sin, but for sin itself as committed against God. Hell is full of remorse, but only for the punishment incurred. There is no real contrition. The rich man uttered not a word of sorrow for his sin against God. (Luke 16:29-30.) But David, though guilty of both murder and adultery, saw his sin as against God alone. (Psalm 51:4.) Mere remorse is not true Godly sorrow unto repentance. Judas though filled with remorse never repented.

Now God alone is able to bestow a contrite and broken heart, a sorrow that will result in the confession and forsaking of sin. And nothing short of that will suffice. "The sacrifices of God are a broken spirit: a broken and a contrite heart, O God, thou wilt not despise." (Psalm 51:17.) "He that covereth his sins shall not prosper: but whoso confesseth and forsaketh them shall have mercy." (Prov. 28:13.) "Only acknowledge thine iniquity, that thou hast transgressed against the Lord thy God." (Jer. 3:13.)

There are three kinds of confession that must be considered :--

(1) Private Confession; for where the sin has been committed against God alone it need be confessed to no other but God. (1 John 1:9; Psalm 32:5.)

(2) Personal Confession; for where the sin has been committed against another it must be confessed not only to God but also to the one who has been wronged. Nor will there be any peace until the confession has been made and forgiveness sought. (Matthew 5:23,24.)

(3) Public Confession; for where the sin has been committed against the church, that is to say, the entire congregation, a class, organization or company of people

the confession must be as public as the transgression. As long as iniquity among the people of God is covered over and unconfessed just so long will the Spirit of God be unable to bring about a Revival. Men must get right with each other in order to be right with God.

One night at the close of a searching message, a young man walked to the front, and, turning to the congregation, made the startling confession that he had stolen and used money that did not belong to him; after which he passed into the inquiry room to get right with God. He had been the treasurer of two important organizations and had squandered nearly all the funds entrusted to him.

It is a common experience to find souls kneeling at the altar and calling upon God with apparent great anguish of heart, who fail to receive anything. And it is just as common for groups of people to gather together for nights of prayer for a Revival and yet never have their prayers answered. What is the trouble? Let the Word of God answer: "Your iniquities have separated between you and your God and your sins have hid His face from you, that He will not hear." Hence, let us uncover our sin first of all; let us make straight the crooked ways, let us gather out the stones, and then we may ask in faith and expectancy for showers of blessing.

Now let us take our sins one by one and deal with each transgression separately. And let us ask ourselves the following questions. It may be we are guilty and God will speak to us.

HCA Board of Directors

Cory Robinson, Chairman
Kathy Moss, Vice Chairman
David Baker, Secretary
John Courtney
Stacey Warbington
Dr. Steve Parr
Tim Rine

HCA Elementary Faculty

Wendy Boyd

Natalie Coker

Kim Collins

Christie Cooksey

Susan Cordle

Meredith Drake

Ben Drust

Linda Dussling

Amy Farley

Michele Forster

Maranda Garrett

Tania Garrett

Michele Holliday

Stephanie Humphrey

Angie Jackson

Ann Jernigan

Karen Lucas

Patty Mapes

Linda Martin

Moises Medina

Megan Sprout

Jenny Stancel

Kate Stinespring

Belinda Wellham

Tammy Whitworth

PJ Wyman

(1) Have we forgiven everyone? Is there any malice, spite, hatred or enmity in our hearts? Do we cherish grudges; and have we refused to be reconciled?

(2) Do we get angry? Are there any uprisings within? Is it true that we still lose our tempers? Does wrath hold us at times in its grip?

(3) Is there any feeling of jealousy? When another is preferred before us does it make us envious and uncomfortable? Do we get jealous of those who can pray, speak and do things better than we can?

(4) Do we get impatient and irritated? Do little things vex and annoy, or, are we sweet, calm and unruffled under all circumstances?

(5) Are we offended easily? When people fail to notice us and pass by without speaking does it hurt? If others are made much of and we are neglected how do we feel about it?

(6) Is there any pride in our hearts? Are we puffed up, do we think a great deal of our own position and attainments?

(7) Have we been dishonest? Is our business open and above reproach? Do we give a yard for a yard and a pound for a pound? Are we honest in our statements. or do we exaggerate and thus convey false impressions?

(8) Have we been gossiping about people? Do we slander the character of others? Are we talebearers and busybodies?

(9) Do we criticize unlovingly, harshly, severely? Are we always finding fault and looking for the flaws in others?

(10) Do we rob God? Have we stolen time that belongs to Him? Has our money been withheld?

(11) Are we guilty of the sin of unbelief? In spite of all He has done for us do we still refuse to believe the promises of His Word?

(12) Have we committed the sin of prayerlessness? Are we intercessors? Do we pray? How much time are we spending on our knees? Have we crowded prayer out of our lives?

(13) Are we neglecting God's Word? How many chapters do we read each day? Are we Bible students? Do we draw our source of supply from the Scriptures?

(14) Are we burdened for the salvation of souls? Have we a love for the lost? Is there any compassion in our hearts for those who are perishing?

(15) Have we failed to confess Christ openly? Are we ashamed of Jesus? Do we keep our mouths closed when we are surrounded by worldly people? Are we witnessing daily?

(16) Are our lives filled with lightness and frivolity? Is our conduct unseemly? Would the world by our actions consider us on its side?

(17) Have we wronged any one and failed to make restitution? Or, has the spirit of Zacchaeus possessed us? Have we restored the many little things that God has shown us?

(18) Are we worried or anxious? Do we fail to trust God for our temporal and spiritual needs? Are we continually crossing bridges before we come to them?

(19) Are we guilty of lustful thoughts? Do we allow our minds to harbor impure and unholy imaginations?

These are the things both negative and positive that prevent the work of God in the midst of His people. Let us be honest and call them by their right name. "SIN" is the word that God uses. And the sooner we admit that we have sinned and are ready to confess and forsake it the sooner may we expect God to hear us and work in mighty power. Why deceive ourselves? We cannot deceive God. Then let us remove the obstacle, the hindering thing before we take another step. "If we would judge ourselves we should not be judged." "Judgment must begin at the house of God."

This has been the history of revival work all down the centuries. Night after night sermons have been preached and no results obtained, until some elder or deacon bursts out in an agony of confession and going to the one whom he has wronged craves forgiveness. Or some woman who is a prominent worker breaks down and in tears confesses publicly that she has been gossiping about some other sister or is not on speaking terms with the person across the aisle. Then when confession and restitution have been made, the fallow ground broken up, sin uncovered and acknowledged, then and not until then, the Spirit of God comes upon the audience and a Revival sweeps over the community.

Generally there is but one sin, one hindering thing. It was an Achan in the camp of Israel. And God will put His finger directly on the spot. Nor will He take it off until that one obstacle has been dealt with.

Oh, then, let us plead first of all the prayer of David when he cried, "Search me, oh God, and see if there be any wicked way in me." And no sooner will the obstacle of sin be taken out of the way than God will come in mighty revival power.

CHAPTER VII FAITH

FAITH is the key that unlocks the door of God's power. "By faith the walls of Jericho fell down." And in revival work one of the indispensable prerequisites is a living, vital Faith. "All things are possible to him that believeth."

The man who is to be used of the Lord will hear from Heaven. God will give him a promise. Not the general promises of the Word that apply to so many of His children, but a definite, unmistakable message direct to his own heart. Some familiar promise, it may be, will suddenly grip him in such a way that he will know God has spoken. Hence, if I would attempt new work for God let me ask myself first of all the question: "Have I a promise?" Has God spoken?"

It was this divine assurance that enabled the prophets of old to go to the people and declare, "Thus saith the Lord." And until God has so commissioned us, we had better remain on our faces in prayer lest He say: "Woe to the prophets that run, and I have not sent them!" But when a man has heard from God, then, "though it tarry, wait for it; because it will surely come." And even should years intervene yet will God fulfil His Word.

And oh, the joy of hearing and recognizing that voice! What encouragement! What faith! How the heart leaps within! No questioning then. No guessing and wondering after that. For days, for weeks it may be, there has been the earnest pleading in prayer as to God's will. Then from His Word, or by the Holy Spirit there comes His message, and all is perfect rest. Not that the thing is done or the expectation realized; but God has spoken, and there can no longer be any doubt. "He will bring it to pass."

I saw, in days gone by, a vision of a great work in the city of Toronto, and I prayed about it that I might know the mind of the Lord. At last one day He spoke. Yea, a second time came His assuring Word. Forthwith I waited, waited in prayer and faith knowing that He would surely bring it to pass. Three years went by, years of fearful testing. Without His promise I would have gone down, my high hopes scattered to the winds, but God had spoken, and I had only to pray: "Do as thou hast said." Finally when three full years had passed, He established the work of which He had spoken.

An incident is told of a place called Filey in the early days of Methodism, to which preacher after preacher had been sent, but all to no purpose. The village was a stronghold of Satanic power, and each one in turn had been driven out until at last it was decided to give it up as a hopeless task.

Just before the matter was finally settled, however, the now famous John Oxtoby, or "Praying Johnny" as he was called, begged the Conference to send him, and so let the people have one more chance. They agreed, and a few days afterwards John set out on his journey. On the way a person who knew him inquired where he was going. "To Filey," was the reply, "where the Lord is going to revive His work."

As he drew near the place, on ascending the hill between Muston and Filey, suddenly a view of the town burst upon his sight. So intense were his feelings that he fell upon his knees under a hedge and wrestled and wept and prayed for the success of his mission. We have been told that a miller, who was on the other side of the hedge, heard a voice and stopped in astonishment to listen, when he heard Johnny say "Thou munna mak a feal o' me! Thou munna mak a feal o' me! I told them at Bridlington that Thou was going to revive Thy work, and Thou must do so, or I shall never be able to show my face among them again, and then what will the people say about praying and believing?"

He continued to plead for several hours. The struggle was long and heavy, but he would not cease. He made his very weakness and inefficiency a plea. At length, the clouds dispersed, the glory filled his soul, and he rose exclaiming, 'It is done, Lord. It is done. Filey is taken. Filey is taken.'

And taken it was, and all in it, and no mistake. Fresh from the Mercy-seat he entered the place, and commenced singing up the streets, "Turn to the Lord and seek salvation," etc. A crowd of stalwart fishermen flocked to listen. Unusual power attended his address, hardened sinners wept, strong men trembled, and while he prayed over a dozen of them fell on their knees, and cried aloud for mercy and found it."

Well now, do we know what it is to offer the prayer of Faith? Have we ever prayed thus? "I knew a father," writes Chas. G. Finney, "who was a good man, but had erroneous views respecting the prayer of faith; and his whole family of children were grown up, without one of them being converted. At length his son sickened, and seemed about to die. The father prayed, but the son grew worse, and seemed sinking into the grave without hope.

The father prayed, until his anguish was unutterable. He went at last and prayed (there seemed no prospect of his son surviving) so that he poured out his soul as if he would not be denied, till at length he got an assurance that his son would not only live but be converted; and that not only this one, but his whole family would be converted to God. He came into the house, and told his family his son would not die. They were astonished at him. 'I tell you,' said he, 'he will not die. And no child of mine will ever die in his sins.' That man's children were all converted years ago."

"A clergyman once told me of a revival among his people, which commenced with a zealous and devoted woman in the Church. She became anxious about sinners, and gave herself to praying for them; she prayed, and her distress increased; and she finally came to the minister, and talked with him, asking him to appoint an anxious inquirers' meeting, for she felt that one was needed. The minister put her off, for he felt nothing of any such need. The next week she came again, and besought him again to appoint such a meeting. She knew there would be somebody to come, for she felt as if God was going to pour out His Spirit. The minister once more put her off. And finally she said to him: 'If you do not appoint the meeting I shall die, for there is certainly going to be a revival.' The next Sabbath he appointed a meeting, and said that if there were any who wished to converse with him about the salvation of their souls, he would meet them on such an evening. He did not know of one, but when he went to the place, to his astonishment he found a large number of anxious inquirers."--(Chas. G. Finney.)

"The first ray of light that broke in upon the midnight which rested on the Churches in Oneida County, in the fall of 1825 was from a woman in feeble health, who, I believe, had never been in a powerful revival. Her soul was exercised about sinners. She was in an agony for the land. She did not know what ailed her, but she kept praying more and more, till it seemed as if her agony would destroy her body. At length she became full of joy. and exclaimed: 'God has come! God has come! There is no mistake about it, the work is begun, and is going all over the region.' And sure enough the work began, and her family were all converted, and the work spread all over that part of the country."-- (Chas. G. Finney.)

The story is told of an invalid who formed the habit of praying for a Revival, daily, for some thirty towns and communities, and from time to time made this entry in his diary: "I was enabled to pray the prayer of faith for __ today." After his death Revivals swept over each of these thirty places, almost exactly in the order he had noted them down. God had spoken, and though he did not live to see any of the answers, yet he was given the assurance that he had been heard.

This then is the secret- Faith, the Faith of Hebrews eleven, the Faith of God, His Gift. based on His Word direct to the heart of His servant. Such Faith will remove mountains, and accomplish the impossible. Not the presumptuous faith that believes without the evidence of the Spirit, and costs nothing, and then when time elapses and things do not come to pass rapidly fades away; but the Faith of God which has been born in the agony of prevailing prayer and soul travail. This Faith will rise above the storms of discouragement and adversity, will triumph over time, and continue to burn brightly while waiting for the accomplishment of its object. Oh, for such a Faith today !

"Faith, mighty faith, the promise sees,

And looks to God alone;

Laughs at impossibilities

And cries, 'It shall be done !'

"The thing surpasses all my thought;

But faithful is my Lord;

Through unbelief I stagger not,

For God hath spoke the word.

"That mighty faith on me bestow

Which cannot ask in vain:

Which holds and will not let Thee go,

Till I my suit obtain."

CHAPTER VIII HEART YEARNINGS FOR REVIVAL

IT was in the years 1917 and 1918 that the yearnings for revival expressed in these messages were born of God. Nothing of a spectacular nature took place for the work was of a wholly local character, nor did it seem to reach full fruition at the time. It was, however, a wonderful personal preparation for the ministry that was to follow, nor will the experiences of those days ever be forgotten.

Perhaps the most profitable way to tell the story will be to simply quote from my diary which was kept day by day at the time. Space forbids a full account. It is only possible to select portions here and there, but these, I believe, will be sufficient to stir up a spirit of revival and thus glorify God.

AUGUST 16Th

It must come, the revival for which I have prayed so long. How God melted me this morning! How sweet is prayer! Praise His name! Oh, for Holy Spirit conviction and Holy Spirit fruit! Only that will stand the test of time and eternity. God has stirred my heart in an unusual way. How unspeakably precious He is. Oh, for conviction, old-fashioned conviction of sin!

Thanks be to God for these wonderful books! How they have helped me! My preaching has been revolutionized. Have been reading them hour after hour. Never got hold of anything like them in my life before: "An Alarm to Unconverted Sinners," by Joseph Alleine; "The Anxious

Inquirer After Salvation," by John Angell James; and "A Call to the Unconverted," by Richard Baxter. These are the books. How clear and definite their message on Sin, Salvation, Heaven and Hell! Yet I realize that even these truths may be proclaimed without results unless there is the power of the Spirit. He must convict. "Not by might, nor by power, but by My Spirit, says the Lord of hosts." And this is perhaps the secret of failure. Truth is preached most earnestly and faithfully but nothing happens. What is the matter? No power.

During my intercession this morning I read a few chapters from "Memoirs of John Smith," by Richard Treffry, and it drove me to prayer. For some time God gave wonderful liberty, perhaps an hour, possibly less. I don't know for I was entirely unconscious of time. And first He led me to confession. Oh, how I have failed! Failed in prayer, for I have spent minutes when I ought to have spent hours. Failed in Bible Study for I have not poured over the sacred pages as I ought. Failed in time for I have allowed Satan to fill my life with other things and thus crowd God out. Failed in service for I have not given out Gospel tracts to the unsaved, nor spoken to them personally about their souls, nor preached on the street corners to the hundreds who do not attend church. Oh, I have failed miserably, miserably failed. And I long to be true and faithful. I plead for souls, yet my eyes do not weep as His did.

But glory be to God, I believe He is leading me into a deeper experience where I will count all things but loss for Christ; where I will suffer, sacrifice, pray, study and serve as never before; where there will be but one thing in my life, and thus the revival for which I long will come.

He will pour forth His Spirit, souls will be convicted and saved. May God hear and graciously answer! I must not fail again. God help me to press on, and on, and on.

AUGUST 25th

In my reading this morning my attention was specially drawn to the following verse: "Herod feared John, knowing that he was a righteous and holy man" (Mark 6:20). Oh, the power of a holy life! Wicked men fear and tremble in the presence of holiness. May God make this an incentive to me. I am reading the New Testament through rapidly for the purpose of selecting those truths which will bring conviction when preached in Holy Spirit power. God is giving searching messages on Sin, Salvation, Heaven and Hell. Spent an hour in prayer and had sweet fellowship. May He lead me on. I want to know and experience more. Never will I be satisfied until God works in convicting power and men and women weep their way to the Cross.

AUGUST 26TH

His message to me this morning was, "All things are possible to him that believeth," and, "This kind can come out by nothing save by prayer" (Mark 9:23, 29). Prayer and faith are both necessary for results and thus the power of Satan will be broken in the hearts of men and Holy Spirit fruit produced. "Lord, I believe; help Thou mine unbelief."

Gathered three into my study this evening. Expected others but they did not come. Talked to them for about an hour. Found much sympathy and willingness to cooperate, but almost entire ignorance as to Holy Spirit fruit and the outpouring of God's Spirit. Decided to meet again along with others to talk it over that we may pray intelligently. Came home rejoicing for I firmly believe that God will move upon the hearts of the people in answer to prevailing prayer.

AUGUST 31st

Eight gathered in the church study tonight and we talked and prayed until after ten. Much prayer had been offered that His Spirit might open their eyes and let them see the need and feel the responsibility. If God has chosen them they will stand with me; if not, I will have to go on alone. We have decided to hold cottage prayer meetings, one each week to begin with. In closing I gave them this verse over which we prayed: "If my people, which are called by my name, shall humble themselves, and pray, and seek my face, and turn from their wicked ways; then will I hear from heaven, and will forgive their sin, and will heal their lad" (2 Chron. 7:14).

SEPTEMBER 2nd

Preached tonight on: "Why you should be saved." Had liberty and a little power. People at great tension. Much prayer, but searched the faces in vain for signs of soul anguish and distress. Eyes dry. No outward token of conviction. Surely I am not yet endued with power from on high. If so there would be Holy Spirit fruit.

SEPTEMBER 7th

"We have toiled all the night and have taken nothing" (Luke 5:1-11). But when they let down their nets under Divine leadership "they enclosed a great multitude of fishes." Has this been my experience, or do I labor in the flesh instead of in the Spirit? Truly I "have toiled all the night and taken nothing." If men do not tremble and go away distressed and broken it is my fault. I must take the blame. When I agonize and travail over souls there will be results, but not before. Then to my knees and on my face until the power comes and God can manifest Himself. Prayed nearly all afternoon, but not much freedom. Heavens like brass.

SEPTEMBER 9th

"But we will give ourselves continually to prayer and to the ministry of the Word" (Acts 6: 4). Once again it must be that I have preached in the flesh and not in the Spirit. Had much liberty and power and felt that there was considerable conviction. The people listened most attentively and there was a great deal of discussion afterwards. Yet nothing happened. None were broken. No distress manifested; no soul anguish; no tears. Oh, for God's power! Luke 24:49; Acts 1: 8; Zech. 4:6; John 6:63. He has chosen me that I should bring forth fruit, fruit that will remain and stand the test of time and eternity (John 15:16). Yet I am not doing it. There is but little fruit. However it sends me to my knees. There must still be hours of waiting upon God. The price has to be paid. And when the Spirit comes upon me and fills me I will know it by the evidence of Holy Spirit fruit. Short of this I dare not rest.

SEPTEMBER 10th

Glory be to God! There has been a move at last. It occurred in the cottage prayer meeting tonight. The service at first was cold and the people unresponsive. I spoke on prevailing prayer, concluded and closed. But no sooner was the meeting over than a woman suddenly cried out: "Pray for me, a church member--" and the rest was drowned in a flood of tears, great mighty sobs that shook her whole body. There was no let up, nor could we speak. She sobbed and sobbed as though her heart would break. Down we went on our knees and prayed one after another. Then we sang, "Just As I Am," and in about fifteen or twenty minutes she came through gloriously saved. Blessed be the name of the Lord!

Oh, how our hearts thrilled with joy. Scarcely could we speak. All the way home in the street car I could hardly contain myself. Only two meetings and God had come. Prayer was answered. The Holy Spirit had commenced to work, for one soul at least had been broken up. A church member unsaved! I wonder how many others are in a like condition ?

SEPTEMBER 12th

God is surely working. Another young woman who had been convicted got up tonight and testified that she was saved yesterday at her work and received full assurance this morning. Praise God! He has again answered prayer. She says she has done almost nothing else but pray all week. So now we have two brought in through the power of God alone. It is for this I have been burdened, the coming of the Holy Spirit in such mighty convicting power that souls would cry out for mercy without even an invitation. God has set His seal and honored His truth. Lord keep me humble and teach me Thy will.

SEPTEMBER 16th

Spoke tonight and had unusual liberty and power. People listened intently. Many eyes were filled with tears, but there was no break. However, I am convinced that God is preparing His servants and that He will yet manifest His power in the conversion of others. It only means that I must spend many more hours in prayer this week than last.

SEPTEMBER 18th

Powerful cottage prayer meeting. House full, prayer fervent. Many hungry for God. Meeting continued until nearly ten o'clock, yet no visible sign. I must experience God's power no matter what it costs. Oh, that He would break me down and cause me to weep for the salvation of souls!

SEPTEMBER 19th

Another break tonight. A backslider tried to pray in the meeting but immediately broke down and wept out her confession. She continued to pray in broken syllables weeping at the same time. Thank God for this, but oh, for an intensified effect! Am still far from satisfied.

Another who has had a terrible struggle asked me tonight if she must confess having stolen something. So God is working.

SEPTEMBER 21st

Received a letter this morning from one in great distress and went to see her at once. Found her weeping in anguish of spirit. After prayer God wonderfully met her and it was good to see the glow of joy in her eyes when leaving. God is surely working with her. Praise His name! More and more I feel the need of prayer.

SEPTEMBER 22nd

Have just finished reading, "Glimpses of Life in Soul-Winning," by James Caughey. Oh, what passion, what devotion and wholehearted earnestness, and what a record of souls saved. Months of battling in prayer, then the victory. I do not believe that there is power enough on earth or in Hell to prevent a revival if I am willing to pay the price.

SEPTEMBER 23rd

After service this morning a lady came to me and said she wanted to become a Christian. We talked and prayed together. She left with a hope but I want to wait and see. Do not know yet whether it is Holy Spirit fruit or not.

SEPTEMBER 24th

Went today to the home of my friend, Dr. E. Ralph Hooper the beloved physician, and had a couple of hours with him in prayer. Was greatly discouraged over last night's service. Things seemed as dead as stone. No liberty, no power, no freedom to preach. Everything was hard. Feel I am just playing with prayer. Must spend more time in intercession.

SEPTEMBER 25th

Three of us met this morning and prayed for four hours. Experienced much blessing. Yet at the cottage prayer meeting tonight there did not seem to be a move of any kind. Two or three confessed sin, while one young man broke out and prayed.

Have been greatly impressed with Joel 2:18 and 28-29. There it is, the need, the methods, and then the results of a great revival. But I can't do it myself. My heart is cold and hard. I do not weep and mourn. May God melt and break me and then work mightily among the people. I found Jer. 5:14 also a great and precious promise and have prayed it on my knees: "I will make my Words in thy mouth fire, and this people wood and it shall devour them." God grant that it may be so.

Glorious break tonight. The prayer meeting seemed cold and dead. Very few prayed. I spoke and closed the meeting disappointed. Then a woman started to weep. She was followed by another and later on a third was broken by God's power. All gathered around and prayed. The first two sobbed and sobbed as though their hearts would break, praying and confessing by turns. Oh, it was glorious. God was working mightily. One of them who had stubbornly refused to pray in public the first night and who had sat throughout the meeting utterly unmoved, now wept so bitterly that she was unable to speak. Finally all went home fully satisfied, the light of heaven in their faces.

I saw that a fourth was under conviction as the result of what had just taken place. She is one of our prominent members. I simply shook hands with her, feeling that it would be best to leave her alone and let the Holy Spirit do His own work. As she passed out there was a look of anguish on her face and her handshake told the story. How wonderfully God uses conversions to bring conviction upon others. Can it be that the revival has started?

Once again I have cause to glory in God. He has given another sign of His presence and power. One other has been convicted and saved and is today rejoicing in God. Six weeks I think it has taken. Now she is free. God has brought her into clear and abiding liberty. In the meeting tonight she testified, her one time dejected face shining with the light of heaven as she told how she had found the peace which passes understanding, saying it was worth all the struggle. Praise God! I believe the work is genuine.

Another also testified, but confessed that she had wandered and grown cold. She knew that she was not right and asked to be prayed for. She did not get through however. There must be deeper conviction. Apparently she has been in a false experience and as a result the work has come undone.

OCTOBER 4th

Spent this afternoon in prayer on my face before God. Then went to Dr. Hooper's home for the evening where we continued in prayer until a quarter to twelve. Oh, for the power of God! We must have it. How wonderfully He opened His Word to us while in prayer. We have read it and prayed it on our knees, especially the second chapter of Joel. Oh, for a baptism of tears! Also the ninth chapter of Daniel. Sentence by sentence we prayed it out before the Lord. We are surrounded by mountains of unbelief and opposition on every side. Only the power of God can overthrow them. "Have faith in God." I want to be wholly absorbed in Him. One passion--Christ.

Lately I have been reading Robert Murray McCheyne, George Fox, Billy Bray, Chas. G. Finney, Henry Moorehouse, John Fletcher, George Whitfield, David Stoner, Henry Martyn, John Wesley, John Bunyan, Thos. Collins, James Caughey, John Smith, David Brainerd; and oh, what men of God they were! What examples of devotion, zeal and piety! Would I could be like them! What a wonder was Wm. Bramwell! But where am I? Oh, to burn out for God! All, all for Him. Jesus only. Souls! Souls! Souls! I am determined to be a winner of souls. God help me.

OCTOBER 5th

Once again, thanks be to God, there has been another conversion. This time a man. He came into my study tonight and told me that he had been convicted in a previous meeting and was most miserable. He had made resolutions again and again and had even tried religion but was still unsaved although he was a member of the church. Yesterday he threw his pipe away. I prayed with him and then we went into the service. Near the close of the meeting he stood up and confessed to all what he had already related to me. His eyes were filled with tears. Yet in spite of this he did not get through. I came home and settled down to pray for him most definitely, pleading with God to let him see the light and enable him to believe.

Faith is rising to assurance. God is working. Deep conviction has already settled upon many. Oh, for a mighty break! Have found Mark 11:22-24; Joel 1:13,14,16; 2:1,11-18, 25, 28, 29, most precious today. Have prayed them one by one before God.

OCTOBER 8th

Very strong opposition. Some of the leading officials object publicly to the meetings. Worldly members up in arms. Satan is beginning to give evidence that he is also interested in what is going on. Have taken it to the Lord in prayer. Continued intercession this evening from about 8 o'clock until a quarter to one in the morning with Dr. Hooper.

OCTOBER 10th

Dr. Hooper and I spent the day waiting on God, and as a result we had a good meeting tonight. Many testified splendidly for over half an hour. Indeed, I had to restrain them in order to give time for prayer. God is working, conviction deepening and spreading. Lives are being changed, souls coming into abundant joy and glorious liberty.

October 11th

God's Word is becoming so precious. We are hearing His voice through the prophets of the Old Testament. Our method is to read a little and then pray it out before God, closing by asking Him to fulfill it in our experience.

"That which is born of the flesh is flesh and that which is born of the Spirit is spirit (John 3:6). If we work in the flesh our fruit will correspond and souls be brought into a false experience. Lord, give us Holy Spirit fruit. We have taken the method of prayer as commanded in God's Word. Every other method has been tried and is being tried today, but the results do not satisfy. So now if we do not prevail in prayer we will become a reproach and to that extent prayer will be discredited. We cannot afford to fail. We must give ourselves continually to prayer and the ministry of the Word. If our lives do not convict people of sin there is something wrong. Oh, for the faith of the Syrophenician woman. She would not take "No" For an answer (Mark 7:24-30).

OCTOBER 14th

Preached morning and night with freedom and liberty, but no apparent result. Am still unsatisfied. Yet God is working a little. A man has restored stolen money to his employer and a woman has given back funds that were taken from the Sunday School as a result of the convicting power of the Spirit. But I pray for the conviction to spread and deepen. Oh, for souls to be wounded! Have been reading the diary of David Brainerd. Months and Months of agonizing prayer and then the mighty power of God upon the Indians. I must have Holy Spirit fruit, nothing less.

CHAPTER IX MANIFESTATIONS OF GOD'S POWER

OCTOBER 17th

DAY by day we have been meeting as usual for prayer. Today we began at 9:30 this morning and continued until after 3:00. We have been asking God to break us for many weeks. About 2:00 this afternoon I was praying when suddenly I stopped and began to praise God. Tears flowed copiously. All I could do was to sob out, "They're lost! They're lost! They're lost!" And so I wept and prayed for the people.

At the meeting tonight, one who had been convicted but had not yet been saved, testified, her face radiant. It was clear that she was genuinely saved and had tasted of the Lord's abounding joy.

OCTOBER 21st

During the past few days the burdens have been very heavy. There is much opposition, but have been burdened in prayer, and some tears have been shed in private for poor perishing souls. Yet how cold is my heart, how little my concern. Oh, for an exhibition of God's power in greater measure, a greater manifestation of His presence!

November 10th

Have had a few precious hours today with Dr. Hooper. Oh, how my heart hungers! Ezra, chapters 8 and 9 have been very precious. Truly, God has opened my eyes to some of the abominations of the Church. But, oh, for a glimpse of my own heart! What abominations must be hidden there! The Lord help me to sigh and cry, for the heathen have come into His inheritance, the Canaanites into the sanctuary.

Everything seems tied up. No more breaks. Work appears to be stopped. But let me to my knees. Results must come. Why should I preach without souls? Lord fulfill Thy Word, begin with some one else. Let something happen. Spirit of God, reveal the hindrance.

NOVEMBER 14th

God has begun with some one else. During the prayer following my message tonight, two broke down and wept. One got through, I believe. The other left under conviction.

NOVEMBER 16th

Another testified tonight. For weeks she has been under conviction, so great that she was afraid to sleep at night, but she is now happy and knows that she is saved.

NOVEMBER 19th

Faith rises. The heavens have seemed like brass, but this afternoon in prayer nothing appeared to be impossible. God is enabling me to believe. O, Lord give me souls. Of what use is preaching if souls are not saved?

It seemed impossible to ask for things this evening. I could only praise and thank Him for all He is going to do. Never have I had such an experience before. The conviction, the certainty that He is working is marvelous.

My Sunday School superintendent has just 'phoned me to say that when he asked a certain person to teach a class she just broke out weeping, saying, she could not because she was not right herself. He prayed with her but she did not get peace. Now he wants me to join him on her behalf. For weeks she confessed she had been under conviction.

NOVEMBER 20th

Am finding God's Word most precious. How it reveals the abominations of my heart!--doubt, unbelief, spiritual pride, coldness, prayerlessness, powerlessness and indifference, as well as the awful abomination of the Church,--the lack of separation, the worldiness of the membership, ungodly choirs, worldly methods of raising money, such as bazaars, concerts, entertainments, etc., the failure to differentiate between the holy and the profane, the clean and the unclean. Do we need a revival? God knows we do. It matters not how holy a church may be, nor how famous as a spiritual center, if souls are not saved, sinners awakened and convicted, there is something radically wrong.

NOVEMBER 21st

At the meeting tonight both the young women for whom we had been pleading came out bright, glorious and clear. They gave splendid testimonies and wept much. Oh, how I praise Him! He is working, convicting and saving. All honor to His name!

DECEMBER 12th

Both of those convicted at the last meeting testified clearly tonight. They are now saved and happy. One has been on our prayer-list just seven days. Praise God!

Spent about three hours in prayer with Dr. Hooper today with much profit.

DECEMBER 19th

Dr. Hooper and I met at eleven this morning and continued in prayer until three in the afternoon. God worked this evening. A young man whom I thought was saved entered my study and astonished me by stating that he had never been born again. This was on Sunday. Tonight he came and sat in the back seat. The doctor and I pleaded long for him in prayer. Had asked God to convict him, to bring him back and cause him to come right out and weep over his sins. I placed three chairs facing the people in the front for the penitent form. At the invitation he walked forward at once and knelt down. Soon he was shaking with great convulsive sobs. Nothing could check them. He pled for mercy and soon knew his sins were pardoned. With tears streaming down his cheeks, he stood up and faced the people and told them that he was saved.

He went home rejoicing in his Saviour. Praise God! He answers prayer. Oh, the joy of soul-winning! The sweetest music I have ever listened to is the cry of a penitent sinner coming home to God. Am determined to cast ease aside and give myself unreservedly to this great work.

JANUARY 9th

After much thought and supplication I set aside this week for prayer and announced a meeting to be held every night except Saturday. Tonight's meeting was truly wonderful. The Holy Spirit so filled one of our number that for the first time in her life she broke out in public prayer. We all felt the power of God. The people refused to go home and so the meeting continued until after eleven o'clock.

JANUARY 11th

This has been the most wonderful week of all. Seldom have our meetings closed until after ten o'clock. The people would not go. God has poured out His Spirit. Conviction has been real. Much soul anguish. Blinded eyes have been opened, sins confessed and put away. Many who never prayed before in public and some whom I thought never could, have broken down and prayed with many tears. The burden for souls has been laid upon several, both young and old. The presence of God has been most real, and oh, what singing! Not the lips only but the hearts.

At the close of the service tonight a quarter after ten, I asked the people, and there was a large attendance, what they wanted done in the future. They were unanimous to continue the meetings. So next week we are to go on again every night. Glory be to God! How graciously He has answered! It is not of man but of Him. God has answered prayer

Prayer has been most difficult all week in spite of God's blessing. Satan seems to be fighting continuously. The heavens have been like brass. This afternoon I went to my study and tried to pray. It was impossible. So hard was I opposed that I finally threw myself down and ceased to struggle, but after awhile I arose determined to win. Then victory came. The powers of darkness seemed to leave and I was enabled to pray for over an hour.

JANUARY 20th

Another wonderful week has passed. The meetings have grown in depth and power. More have been saved.

JANUARY 23rd

A shower at last. Praise be to God! Room packed. During the meeting I was in an agony almost to bursting, so heavy was the burden. At the close I gave an invitation. We sang two verses but no one came. Then we sang, "Like a Mighty Sea," our grand old favorite. During the first two verses I was still in agony. The load lifted as we started the third verse. Oh, how they sang! Soul and heart in every word. But I had given up hope of results. Suddenly a woman came forward and knelt at the front. Soon a second followed. Then two or three others. I stepped up to a fourth who was under deep conviction and spoke only a word or two. Almost immediately her eyes rifled with tears, her head dropped and in a moment she was on her face before God. There were six altogether. Oh, what a night! Finally I dismissed the people and told them to go home, but they still stayed, unwilling to leave. Tears flowed freely, sobs were heard as they wept out their confessions of sin. God worked and soon many had risen to testify of sins forgiven. Oh, the joy that filled our hearts!

MARCH 6th

The work of God still prospers. Souls are saved every week. Wonderful meeting tonight. Last Thursday night a young university student was saved. He came some weeks ago and went away determined he would never come again. Next week he found himself in the meeting once more, much against his will. For weeks he fought but kept coming. God was working with him. Conviction deepened. He was most miserable. Last Thursday night however, he yielded. Another man stood beside him so that he could not get out, but he pushed the chair in front of him away and knelt down before every one. God saved him and we broke out as usual with, "'Tis done, the great transaction's done." Tonight he bore glorious testimony.

MARCH 7th

Another saved tonight. It was her first meeting. She literally sobbed out her prayer. Oh, this a glorious work! To God be the praise!

MARCH 13th

Two more. One, a leading member, exclaimed, "I thought I was a Christian; I have been a member of the church so long, but tonight I see myself a guilty sinner." The other, a woman for whom we have long prayed and who has been under deep conviction and most miserable, came and sought pardon. Both were saved. I myself always thought she was a Christian. Oh, how God works! May He save many more church members who are in a false experience.

MARCH 27th

A very clear exhibition of God's power tonight. A young man standing against the door at the back cried out. The audience was startled. He said he had professed salvation two years ago, but that sin had crept in and he was not right with God. He had spent an awful week, but was determined to get through before he left. He came down the aisle and knelt at the front. God heard and answered. Oh, for more such fruit!

MAY 2nd

The hardest and most discouraging meeting we have yet had. Let a man who doesn't believe in a personal and very real devil begin to pray and work for a revival and he will soon meet the enemy and know something of his resisting powers. Surely he was present last night. Everything was dead and frozen. Nothing would go; neither prayers nor testimonies. I had a message prepared, but could not deliver it. All that I could do was to groan and weep in prayer. At the close of the meeting I announced that I was going to retire to the study to pray. Who followed me I did not know, for I was engaged with God. But I found afterward that there were at least a dozen surrounding me in prayer. It was a hard time. I prayed and broke down in the middle of it and sobbed until I was weak. I was determined to pray through and find out where we were. One by one the people left until at last there were but two of us. Some time after midnight the light slowly broke and many things were revealed. My own failures became apparent. Faith began to rise, and at three o'clock in the morning we left perfectly satisfied, weak in body but strong in faith. The battle had been won, and Satan defeated.

Tonight it was heaven. Oh, how our hearts sang for joy and how near God seemed! Heaven seemed open and faith was, within our grasp. We mounted up as eagles. God gave us full assurance. Nothing seemed impossible. I prayed four times during the meeting and a wonderful spirit of prayer was upon all. Over and over again we sang those glorious words of Wesley's:

"Faith, mighty faith, the promise sees,

And looks to God alone;

Laughs at impossibilities

And cries: 'It shall be done!'"

MAY 17th

This morning in my reading God gave me a precious word from Dent. 2:25. We have been meeting for prayer from 5 and 6 until 10 at night, but I find that Satan is at work as an angel of light. May God make us wise as serpents. Have been reading the diary of David Stoner. How I thank God for it! He is another Brainerd. Have been much helped, but, how ashamed and humble I feel as I read it! Oh, how he thirsted and searched after God! How he agonized and travailed! And he died at thirty-two.

What kind of an experience have I? Am I burdened for lost souls? Do I love to pray? Has my desire for the world gone? Do I hate sin? Am I filled with joy and the love of God? Do I get my prayers answered? Is there any hidden thing, any secret sin, or am I holy in heart and life? Have I spiritual discernment? Am I able to detect a Holy Spirit sermon? Can I tell when people are spiritual? Is my religion real? Do those at home believe in me? Am I truly representing Christ? Will people get a right view of Him from my life? Am I willing to let God search and try me? Is there anything false about my experience? Have I the clear witness of the Holy Spirit? Does my life magnify Jesus Christ? I must pray about these things.

THE CHURCHES

A city full of churches,

Great preachers, lettered men,

Grand music, choirs and organs;

If these all fail, what then?

Good workers, eager, earnest,

Who labour hour by hour:

But where, oh where, my brothers!

Is God's Almighty power?

Refinement: Education!

They want the very best.

Their plans and schemes are perfect,

They give themselves no rest;

They get the best of talent,

They try their uttermost,

But what they need, my brother,

Is God the Holy Ghost!

We may spend time and money

And preach from wisdom's lore,

But education only

Will keep God's people poor.

God wants not worldly wisdom.

He seeks no smiles to win;

But what is needed, brother,

Is that we deal with sin!

It is the Holy Spirit,

That quickeneth the soul.

God will not take man-worship,

Nor bow to man's control.

No human innovation,

No skill, or worldly art,

Can give a true repentance,

Or break the sinner's heart!

We may have human wisdom,

Grand singing, great success;

There may be fine equipment,

But these things do not bless.

God wants a pure, clean vessel,

Anointed lips and true,

A man filled with the Spirit,

To speak His message through.

Great God, revive us truly!

And keep us every day;

That men may all acknowledge

We live just as we pray.

The Lord's hand is not shortened,

He still delights to bless;

If we depart from evil

And all our sins confess.

Samuel Stevenson.

CHAPTER X SPIRITUAL EXPERIENCES OF PRICELESS VALUE

MAY 22nd

IT is coming to me more and more to challenge my work; to test and prove everything. I feel quite certain that one of the outstanding reasons for failure lies in the fact that we do not judge ourselves. I must challenge my preaching. God claims that His Word is a fire, a hammer, and a sword. Now if it not this, then there is something WRONG. God has promised fruit. There must be results. He must make His Word what He says it is. I challenge my prayer life. Have I power to prevail with God? If not, why not? Has God not most emphatically stated that "he shall have whatsoever He saith?" If I pray and do not get answers there must be something wrong. I must challenge my Christian experience. Do I feel any uprisings, any temper? Is there anything contrary to love in my heart? Am I growing in grace and going on with God? Have I complete deliverance from sin? Do my nearest and dearest believe in my religion? Lord judge me, and bring me to a higher level spiritually.

Weeks ago God gave me the gift of faith, and I knew He was going to work, but after a few hours I let it go. Weeks passed and finally on a Thursday afternoon He again gave me the same wonderful gift only far more glorious. For a week I held it in conscious joy, and then once again lost it. Oh, what a failure I am! Why can I not believe God? Has He not said that "all things are possible to him that believeth?" This is where David Stoner failed. Lord, increase my faith.

> "That mighty faith on me bestow
>
> Which cannot ask in vain;
>
> Which holds, and will not let Thee go
>
> Till I my suit obtain."

MAY 24th

Spent the day in prayer and fasting. On Wednesday night at the prayer meeting I announced that we would set aside the holiday when most were in the parks and places of amusement, as a day of prayer and fasting unto God. So we met at nine this morning and prayed through until nine tonight. The time passed very quickly and was a great blessing to many. Our prayer was for an outpouring of God's Spirit. Oh, how the people prayed! "What hath God wrought!"

Have been greatly blessed in reading the story of the glorious Irish revival of 1859.

MAY 26th

Preached tonight on the Judgment. God gave me marvelous liberty. There must have been about a thousand present. The wife of a leading business man was greatly affected. Used her handkerchief [Sic.] freely and finally pulled her veil down to hide her tears. Our leading soloist, for whom we have been praying much, kept her head bowed all through the sermon and appeared to be deeply concerned. Others were also under conviction. Praise be to God for answered prayer! May we continue to "hold the fort" until He comes.

MAY 27th

I have come to the place where I realize that I know almost nothing about experimental religion. I have the "form of Godliness," but not the "power." It is in my head but not in my heart. My religion is theoretical, rather than experimental. Mrs. John Fletcher, Wm. Bramwell, and John Smith had something to which I am a total stranger, As a result of much reading I am convinced that the Early Methodists were nearest to the apostolic experience of any body of people I know. Would to God they had never lost their power! Oh, what God has in store for His saints. Experience it I must, cost what it will. May the Holy Spirit be my teacher as I read, pray and meditate. Oh, for the faith to believe!--the faith of those wonderful men and women of a century or two ago.

MAY 29th

Wonderful meeting! Marvelous exhibition of God's power! Was unable to give the message prepared but spoke with liberty as He led. Conviction very deep. Some quite mad. Six came and knelt at the front without an invitation. One who had been very angry because we prayed for her was deeply moved tonight. She had sworn that she would never come as a penitent, would never bow at the front. But she came, nevertheless. Hallelujah!

JUNE 2nd

We made Saturday our second day of prayer and fasting, pleading with God for eight hours and had a very blessed experience.

Have been reading the marvelous life story of Mrs. Fletcher. How little I know of her wonderful walk with God. Oh, how she suffered! What patience, faith and confidence! It drives me to my knees and I have to cry out as I see my unworthiness. Lord, deliver me from everything that does not glorify Thee. Keep me each moment in Thy will. Give me a little of what John Fletcher possessed. Oh, how I yearn for more! How my heart hungers after righteousness.

JUNE 5th

Wonderful meeting tonight. Four backsliders came and knelt at the front. All got through. The people then began to testify and the singing was deeply spiritual. Finally I said to them, "Don't you want to go home? .... No," they answered from all sides. "Well," I replied, "it is now twenty minutes to eleven." They were amazed. "I wonder," I continued, "if this is the revival?" The joy was very great in many hearts tonight. To Him be all the glory!

I find as we advance spiritually and go deeper that we lose our relish for the lighter and more popular hymns, and develop an amazing love for the grand old standards that were so greatly used of God in other days. Over and over again now we sing, "Come Ye Sinners Poor and Needy," "Oh, Could I Speak the Matchless Worth," "Oh, for a Thousand Tongues to Sing," "Depth of Mercy," "Arise, My Soul, Arise," "Oh, for a Heart to Praise My God," "Oh, Love Divine," "Give Me the Wings of Faith to Rise," "Faith, Mighty Faith."

JUNE 9th

This morning on my way to church the peace of God filled my heart to overflowing. Passage after passage of Scripture came to me and I sang as I walked along. Especially was that verse precious:

"Jesus, the name high over all,

In hell, or earth, or sky;

Angels and men before it fall,

And devils fear and fly."

I wondered at the unusual presence of God and asked myself if such peace could remain in times of trial and persecution. After the service I was greatly encouraged by two who told me of fetters snapped and wonderful blessing received. Trial and bitter opposition followed. Satan is still busy. Even some of our best church members are allowing themselves to be made his tools to hinder the work and put obstacles in the way.

JUNE 18th

While the message was being given tonight a man suddenly rose from his seat and with a deep groan sank down on his knees at the front. The light soon broke and turning to the audience he said: "Well friends. I have found Jesus. I have found Jesus." Oh, the marvelous power of God! How wonderfully He works in answer to the prayer of faith.

This morning I left the house at 6:30. Walked to the church and began to pray at 6:45. But was so weary, tired and sleepy that I laid down after trying in vain for some fifteen minutes to get in touch with God, and slept for an hour and a half. Then at 8:30 I began to pray again and for the next hour and a half I had wonderful liberty and great blessing. God was very near and I believe I was able to prevail. I then had a quiet feast on the Word and noted specially the power of a righteous and holy life.

JUNE 19th

This morning four of us met for prayer from eight to twelve and had a blessed time. At the meeting last Thursday some took exception to what I said and felt that I was complaining, scolding and criticizing because I had urged them to more prayer. But at the service tonight we gathered in a new consecration and there was great joy on many faces. However, it has shown me that it is useless to try to work it up in the flesh, that only God can lay the burden of prayer upon others, and that I must leave it to Him. When people are really burdened by the Holy Spirit they will not require any urging. Thank God, real prayer-helpers have been raised up.

JUNE 21st

There are two verses which have been specially blessed to me lately. The first: "Call unto Me and I will answer and show thee great and mighty things that thou knowest not" (Jer. 33:3). Lord, enable me to grasp it by faith and let me see the "great and mighty things" that I call unto Thee for. And the second: "And they went forth and preached everywhere, the Lord working with them and confirming the Word with signs following" (Mark 16:20). Am I sure that the Lord is working with me? What proof have I unless I see the Word that I preach confirmed by signs following. Am I satisfied to go on without the assurance? I must see conviction of sin culminating in the salvation of souls.

JULY 1st

Spent this day in prayer and fasting along with five or six others whose hearts the Lord has touched. Satan's resistance was strong; nor were we able to pray through and prevail.

AUGUST 5th

The Devil has been busy once more. One man is determined to stop his wife attending the meetings. He was very angry and threatened many things. But a meeting was held in his home upon the invitation of his wife at which he was convicted, brought to see his error and is now convinced that he is not right. Satan does not mind people attending the ordinary church at all, but as soon as his kingdom is invaded he is up in arms at once. There are several who have forbidden their wives attending our meetings.

AUGUST 16th

Looking back in my diary I note that today marks one year since I was first burdened in a special way for a revival. We have made this a day of prayer and have reviewed the year's work before God. Some of the professed converts have gone back, though the majority are standing true. What kind of children have we borne? We must distinguish clearly between the genuine and the counterfeit, between the work of the Spirit and the work of the flesh. May our prayers prevail more than ever. Fruit must not be plucked before it is ripe. We want children who will love their parents, love their home, the place of their birth, and who will always be present at meal time. The other kind are unnatural. Some are going on wonderfully and becoming real prayer helpers.

AUGUST 24th

God is still working and answering prayer. We are seeing some mighty things. The converts are being called upon to suffer persecution. One of them tells of how the people next door ever since the change came into her life have acted as mean as possible, throwing dirty water and rubbish on her pathway and doing everything to make her angry. She never said a word but treated them just the same as she always has. She put one of our tracts in their letter box and believes she read it, for the next day the woman looked daggers at her. Well, the other day the woman was taken very hurriedly to the hospital for an operation. Our convert went to the husband who was very much surprised, and next day visited the woman in the hospital and prayed with her. The woman broke down and sobbed. Next morning the husband came and said, "Do you think the Lord can forgive me for all I have done?"

AUGUST26th

Last week I wrote to George W. Stenton of Peterborough, insisting that he come to help me in prayer. He came and we have had a wonderful time together. This afternoon when I announced that supper was ready he lifted his head from the floor with a look of amazement on his face. His eyes were filled with tears. He looked as though he had been in heaven and had been suddenly hurled to earth again, for he was all melted and broken up. God has given him a great faith and he knows how to hold on in prayer. The answers he receives are amazing. It inspires faith in others for he lives with God.

SEPTEMBER 9th

The Word is becoming more precious to me all the time. I delight in reading chapters from the old prophets. My heart hungers for a fuller experience of God's salvation and a closer walk with Jesus Christ. I want to be weaned from the world and all it contains. The more I pray the more I love to pray. God is my portion.

SEPTEMBER 15th

God has tonight set to His seal, borne witness to the truth, and confirmed His Word. While I was preaching a young woman, who was a stranger, rose to her feet and stood still for some time before I observed her. I stopped speaking, praised God, and asked her if she had decided for Christ. From her answer it appeared that she could not wait until the close of the service so deeply had she been convicted. Then I went on with my sermon. The effect was wonderful. An awe overspread the entire congregation and scores were deeply stirred. As I went on three men and two women were observed weeping. One man sobbed aloud. The young woman who had stood came to my study after the service and so far as I could tell was clear in her pardon. How we praised God!

SEPTEMBER 23rd

There must be more soul-anguish and deeper conviction of sin, but this is wholly the operation of the Spirit. Therefore nothing but the prayer of faith will avail. It is God who saves souls. The work of God is the operation of the Holy Spirit in answer to the prayer of faith. I have read the life of John Smith once again. What a man of prayer and faith he was! And how he aimed for souls! There are many books that describe revival and relate the results of God's work, but John Smith tells me how to get it, how to do it, the method, the only method that produces Holy Spirit fruit and procures an outcome for God's glory.

Am now reading the Journals of John Wesley for the first time. Four large volumes. Will I ever finish them ? I think so for I find them intensely interesting and helpful. Oh, what a man he was! And how wonderfully he proclaimed the great fundamental doctrine of salvation by faith alone.

Work on, Thou Spirit of Power, and raise up once more a people for Thy name! Grant us again a visitation from on High, a return of apostolic days, for surely this is heaven below! And in it all may Jesus Christ be glorified. Amen!

THE REVIVAL HYMN

Revive Thy work, O Lord!

And manifest Thy power;

Oh, come upon Thy Church, and give

A penitential shower!

Revive Thy work, O Lord!

Come now and answer prayer;

Oh, come in Holy Spirit power,

And save men everywhere!

Revive Thy work, O Lord!

And every soul inspire;

Oh, kindle in each heart, we pray,

The pentecostal fire!

Revive Thy work, O Lord!

And give abounding joy;

Oh, fill our hearts with perfect love;

And burn out all alloy!

Revive Thy work, O Lord!

And make Thy servants bold;

Convict of sin, and work once more

As in the days of old.

Revive Thy work, O Lord!

Fulfill Thy promise true;

Let Jesus Christ be glorified,

And great things for us do.

Oswald J. Smith

Together for JESUS
    Orchestra — playing in tune and in time
        TEAM   w/ the power of the Holy Spirit
                    working in the lives of those
                    we serve. —

                    leading people to life-changing faith
                        in Jesus
        making disciples
                    — outward
                    — death — life
                    —

            for the glory of God. — Solely God.